Peter Bilhorn

Crowning glory

For use in the church

Peter Bilhorn

Crowning glory
For use in the church

ISBN/EAN: 9783337269289

Printed in Europe, USA, Canada, Australia, Japan

Cover: Foto ©Lupo / pixelio.de

More available books at **www.hansebooks.com**

CROWNING GLORY

≫ REVISED ≪

FOR USE IN

The Church, Evangelistic Meetings, Sunday School, Young People's Societies, and the Home,

BY

P. P. Bilhorn.

PUBLISHED BY

BILHORN BROTHERS,

GARDEN CITY BLOCK, · · · N. W. Cor. Randolph & 5th Ave., · · · ROOMS 716 & 717,

CHICAGO, ILL.

Price, by Mail, 35cts. per Copy. By Express, not prepaid, $3.60, per Dozen. $30.00 per Hundred.
THIS BOOK IS CLOTH BOUND.

PREFACE.

AFTER months of most careful and prayerful study these Hymns are sent out through the land with the prayer that God may use them for His own glory in the upbuilding of Christians and the winning of souls to Christ.

Many of the hymns, both words and music, were written in the very midst of great religious awakenings, and to meet the needs we have felt in our own work: and all of them, we believe, will sing their way into the hearts of Christians, everywhere.

We have tested them all. We have called upon our friends for criticism, and more than all, we have given them unto Him in whose name we preach and sing; and believing it is His will that the Book should go forth, we set it singing His praises, who loved us and gave Himself for us.

J. Wilbur Chapman.

P. P. Bilhorn.

Examine carefully the binding, print and paper.

CROWNING GLORY

REVISED

No. 1. **Revive Us Again.**

Dr. W. P. Mackay.   English Melody.

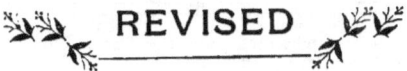

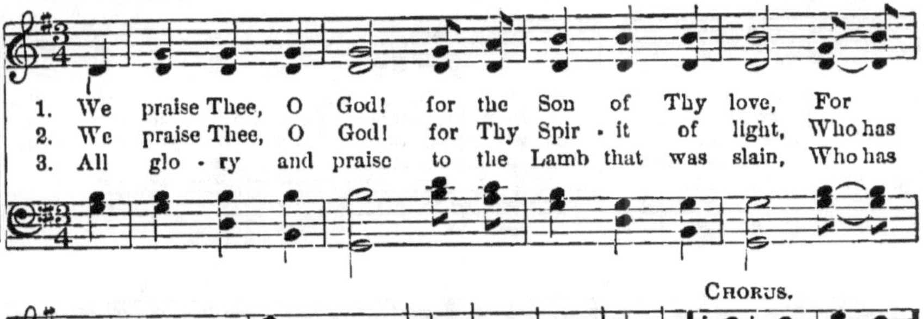

1. We praise Thee, O God! for the Son of Thy love, For
2. We praise Thee, O God! for Thy Spir-it of light, Who has
3. All glo-ry and praise to the Lamb that was slain, Who has

CHORUS.

Je-sus who died, and is now gone a-bove. Hal-le-lu-jah!
shown us our Sav-ior, and scat-tered our night. Hal-le-lu-jah!
borne all our sins, and has cleansed ev-'ry stain. Hal-le-lu-jah!

Thine the glo-ry, Hal-le-lu-jah! A-men. Re-vive us a-gain.

4. All glory and praise to the God of all grace,
   Who has bought us, and sought us, and guided our ways.

5. Revive us again; fill each heart with Thy love;
   May each soul be rekindled with fire from above.

No. 3. Go Forth! Go Forth!

L. E. Jones.   P. P. Bilhorn.

1. The field is great, the grain is white, The day is fad-ing in-to night;
2. Go forth, and reap with will-ing hands, The golden grain a-wait-ing stands;
3. Go forth, the la-bor-ers are few, There's much for will-ing hands to do;

Go forth, go forth, nor i-dle be, The Lord of har-vest need-eth thee.
Go forth, go forth, and gar-ner in The wand'ring ones from paths of sin.
Go forth, go forth, do not de-lay, The Mas-ter bids you haste a-way.

Chorus.

Go forth, go forth and reap to-day, The field is read-y, haste a-way;
Go forth, some pre-cious soul to win, Go bid them quick-ly en-ter in.

No. 6. Redemption.

F. J. Crosby. — Peter Bilhorn.

1. O wonderful words of the Gospel! O wonderful message they bring, Proclaiming a blessed redemption Thro' Jesus our Savior and King.
2. He came from the throne of His glory, And left the bright mansions above, The world to redeem from its bondage; So great His compassion and love.
3. O come to this wonderful Savior, Come weary and sorrow-oppressed, Behold on the cross how He suffered, That you in His kingdom might rest.
4. There's no other refuge but Jesus, No shelter where lost ones may fly; And now, while He's tenderly calling: O "turn ye," "for why will ye die?"

CHORUS.

Believe, oh, believe in His mercy That flows like a fountain so free; Believe, and re-

Redemption. Concluded.

ceive the re-demp-tion He of-fers to you and to me.

No. 7. Fill Me Now.

E. H. Stokes. D. D.   Jno. R. Sweney. By per.

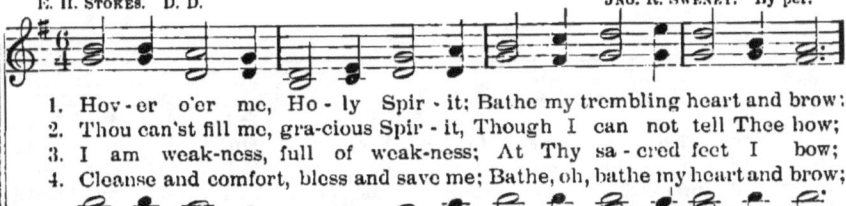

1. Hov-er o'er me, Ho-ly Spir-it; Bathe my trembling heart and brow;
2. Thou can'st fill me, gra-cious Spir-it, Though I can not tell Thee how;
3. I am weak-ness, full of weak-ness; At Thy sa-cred feet I bow;
4. Cleanse and comfort, bless and save me; Bathe, oh, bathe my heart and brow;

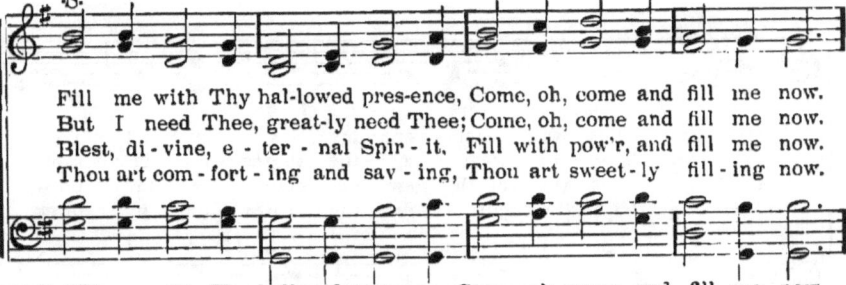

Fill me with Thy hal-lowed pres-ence, Come, oh, come and fill me now.
But I need Thee, great-ly need Thee; Come, oh, come and fill me now.
Blest, di-vine, e-ter-nal Spir-it, Fill with pow'r, and fill me now.
Thou art com-fort-ing and sav-ing, Thou art sweet-ly fill-ing now.

D.S. Fill me with Thy hallow'd presence, Come, oh, come and fill me now.

CHORUS.   D.S.

Fill me now, fill me now, Je-sus, come and fill me now.

No. 8. My Jesus, I love Thee.

"Mine are thine and thine are mine."—John 17:10.

London Hymn Book, 1864.   A. J. Gordon. By per.

1. My Jesus, I love Thee, I know Thou art mine,
   For Thee all the follies of sin I resign;
   My gracious Redeemer, my Saviour art Thou,
   If ever I loved Thee, my Jesus, 'tis now.

2. I love Thee, because Thou hast first loved me,
   And purchased my pardon on Calvary's tree;
   I love Thee for wearing the thorns on Thy brow;
   If ever I loved Thee, my Jesus, 'tis now.

3. I will love Thee in life, I will love Thee in death,
   And praise Thee as long as Thou lendest me breath;
   And say when the death-dew lies cold on my brow,
   If ever I loved Thee, my Jesus, 'tis now.

4. In mansions of glory and endless delight,
   I'll ever adore Thee in heaven so bright;
   I'll sing with the glittering crown on my brow,
   If ever I loved Thee, my Jesus, 'tis now.

No. 11. I Will, I Will!

Rev. E. F. Hallenbeck.   P. P. Bilhorn.

1. O why should I long-er re-ject Him? The way of sal-va-tion is clear;
2. The Sav-ior so lov-ing and ten-der, Stands waiting so close to my side;
3. And now, if I'll on-ly con-fess Him, His peace like a riv-er will flow;
4. Lord Je-sus, I do now ac-cept Thee, My Sav-ior and Shepherd to be;

I'm saved, if I on-ly ac-cept Him: Then why should I fal-ter or fear?
My will un-to Him I sur-ren-der; I'll trust in the Christ cru-ci-fied.
My life will be filled with rich blessing, And that I am saved I shall know.
I'll trav-el life's pathway be-side Thee; I'm saved, and Thy blood is my plea.

CHORUS.   *Cres.*

I will,...... I will,...... I will ac-cept Je-sus now.
    I will,   I will,

I will,...... I will, I will, I will trust the Sav-ior now.
    I will,

Copyright, 1891, by P. P. Bilhorn.

No. 19. I'm Bound to Enter Heaven.

Miss ADA BLENKHORN.
Miss A. BLENKHORN.
Arr. by P. B.

Not too fast. *Faster.*

1. The Sav-ior gave His life for me, I'm bound to en-ter heav-en.
2. O, broth-er won't you come with me, I'm bound to en-ter heav-en.
3. He walks each rug-ged path with me, I'm bound to en-ter heav-en.
4. There waits for me a roy-al crown, I'm bound to en-ter heav-en.
5. To His own word He will be true, I'm bound to en-ter heav-en.

From Sa-tan's yoke He sets me free, I'm bound to en-ter heav-en.
To-day the Sav-ior call-eth thee, O come to en-ter heav-en.
Each thorn-y path He'll walk with thee, O come to en-ter heav-en.
When life's last bur-den I lay down, I'm bound to en-ter heav-en.
He'll keep a star-ry crown for you, O, come and en-ter heav-en.

CHORUS.

Bound for the Ca-naan land, Bound for the Ca-naan land, Bound for the Ca-naan land, I'm bound to en-ter heav-en.

Copyright, 1892, by Peter Bilhorn.

No. 25. Stand up for Jesus.

G. DUFFIELD.   G. J. WEBBE.

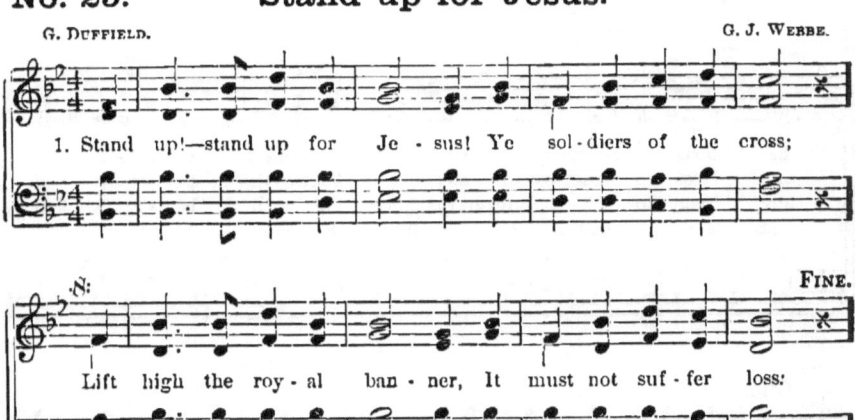

2 Stand up!—stand up for Jesus!
   Stand in His strength alone,
   The arm of flesh will fail you—
   Ye dare not trust your own:
   Put on the gospel armor,
   And, watching unto prayer,
   Where duty calls or danger,
   Be never wanting there.

3 Stand up!—stand up for Jesus!
   The strife will not be long;
   This day the noise of battle,
   The next, the victor's song:
   To him that overcometh,
   A crown of life shall be;
   He with the King of glory
   Shall reign eternally!

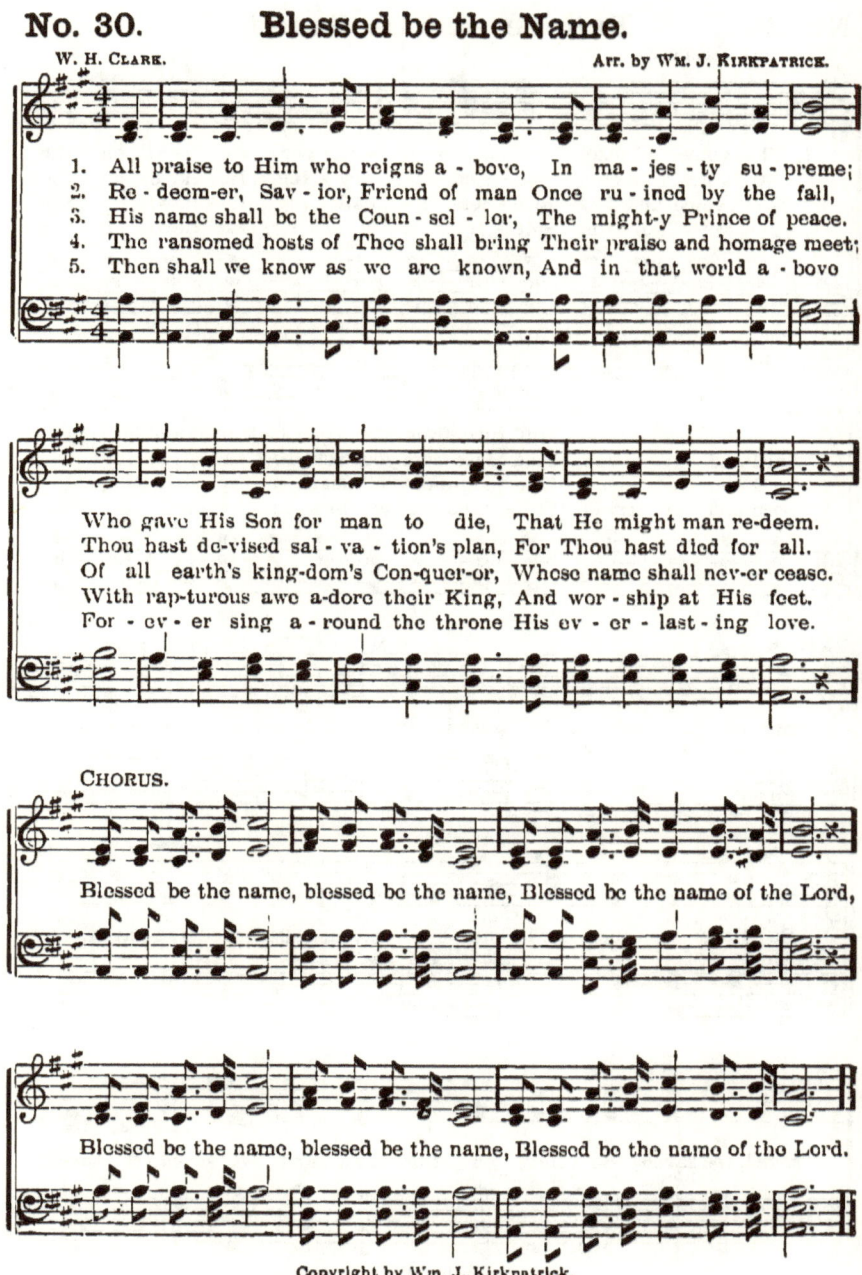

No. 35. How Firm a Foundation.

GEORGE KEITH.   PORTUGUESE HYMN.

1. How firm a foun-da-tion, ye saints of the Lord, Is laid for your faith in his ex-cel-lent word, What more can he say, than to you he hath said, To you, who for re-fuge to Je-sus have fled? To you, who for re-fuge to Je-sus have fled?

2. "Fear not, I am with thee, O be not dis-mayed, For I am thy God, I will still give thee aid; I'll strengthen thee, help thee, and cause thee to stand, Up-held by my gra-cious, om-ni-po-tent hand, Up-held by my gra-cious, om-ni-po-tent hand."

3. "When thro' the deep wa-ters I call thee to go, The riv-ers of sor-row shall not o-ver-flow; For I will be with thee the tri-als to bless, And sanc-ti-fy to thee thy deep-est dis-tress, And sanc-ti-fy to thee thy deep-est dis-tress."

4. "The soul that on Je-sus hath leaned for re-pose, I will not, I will not de-sert to his foes; That soul, though all hell should en-deav-or to shake, I'll nev-er, no nev-er, no nev-er for-sake, I'll nev-er, no nev-er, no nev-er for-sake!"

He Calleth for Thee. Concluded.

God be with You.—Concluded.

meet, God be with you till we meet a-gain.
meet, till we meet, God be with you till we meet a-gain.

No. 42. While Jesus whispers.

"Come unto me, all ye that labor and are heavy laden."—Matt. 9:28.

W. E. WITTER. H. R. PALMER.

1. While Je-sus whis-pers to you, Come, sin-ner, come! While we are
2. Are you too heav-y la-den? Come, sin-ner, come! Je-sus will
3. Oh, hear his ten-der plead-ing, Come, sin-ner, come! Come and re-

pray-ing for you, Come, sin-ner, come! Now is the time to own Him,
bear your bur-den, Come, sin-ner, come! Je-sus will not de-ceive you,
ceive the bless-ing, Come, sin-ner, come! While Je-sus whispers to you,

Come, sin-ner, come! Now is the time to know Him, Come, sin-ner, come!
Come, sin-ner, come! Je-sus can now re-deem you, Come, sin-ner, come!
Come, sin-ner, come! While we are pray-ing for you, Come, sin-ner, come!

Copyright 1879, by H. R. Palmer.

No. 44. Anywhere with Jesus.

"I will trust and not be afraid."—Isaiah 12:2.

Jessie H. Brown.   D. B. Towner.

1. An-y-where with Je-sus I can safe-ly go, An-y-where He leads me in this world be-low. An-y-where with-out Him, dear-est joys would fade, An-y-where with Je-sus I am not a-fraid.
2. An-y-where with Je-sus I am not a-lone, Oth-er friends may fail me, He is still my own. Tho' His hand may lead me o-ver drear-est ways, An-y-where with Je-sus is a house of praise.
3. An-y-where with Je-sus I can go to sleep, When the dark ling shad-ows round a-bout me creep, Know-ing I shall wak-en nev-er more to roam, An-y-where with Je-sus will be home, sweet home.

CHORUS.

An-y-where! an-y-where! Fear I can-not know. An-y-where with Je-sus I can safe-ly go.

By permission of D. B. Towner, owner of copyright.

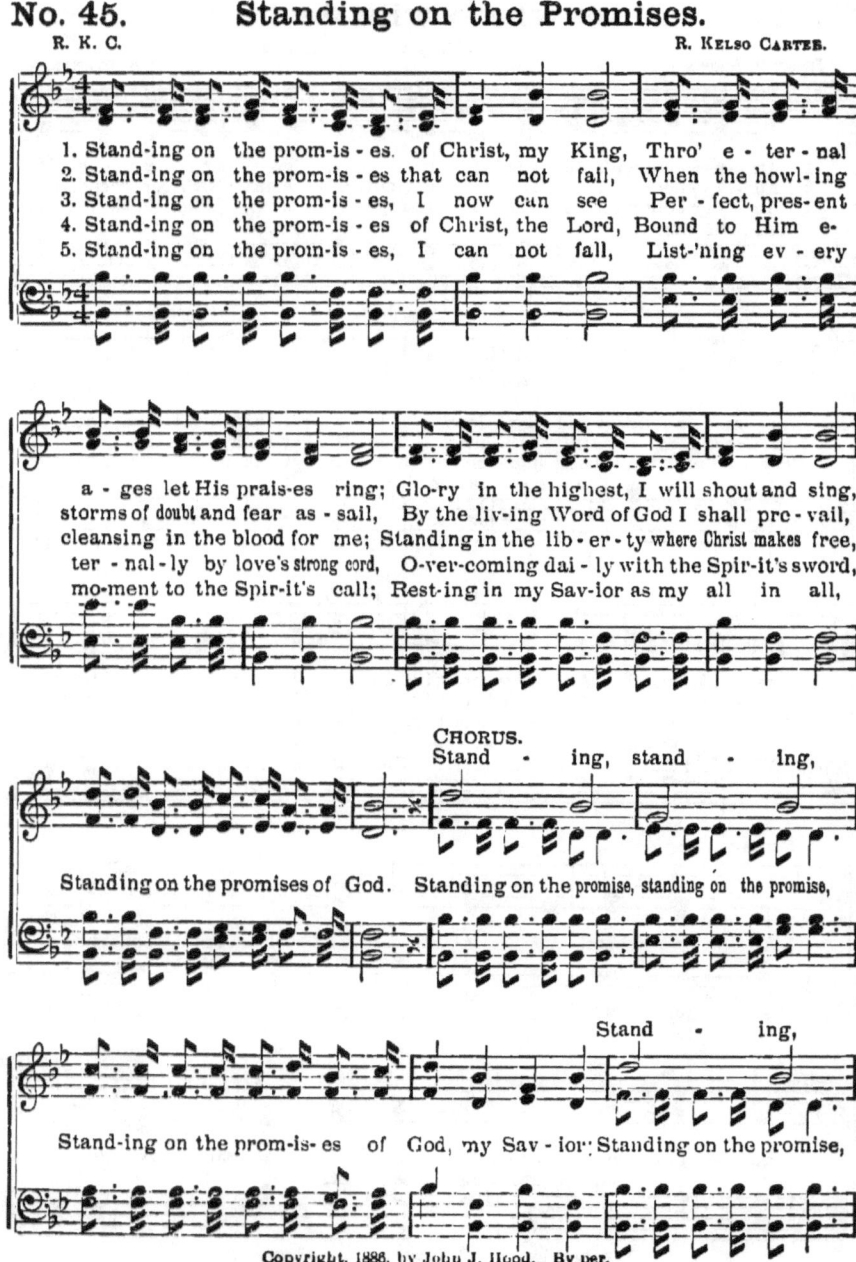

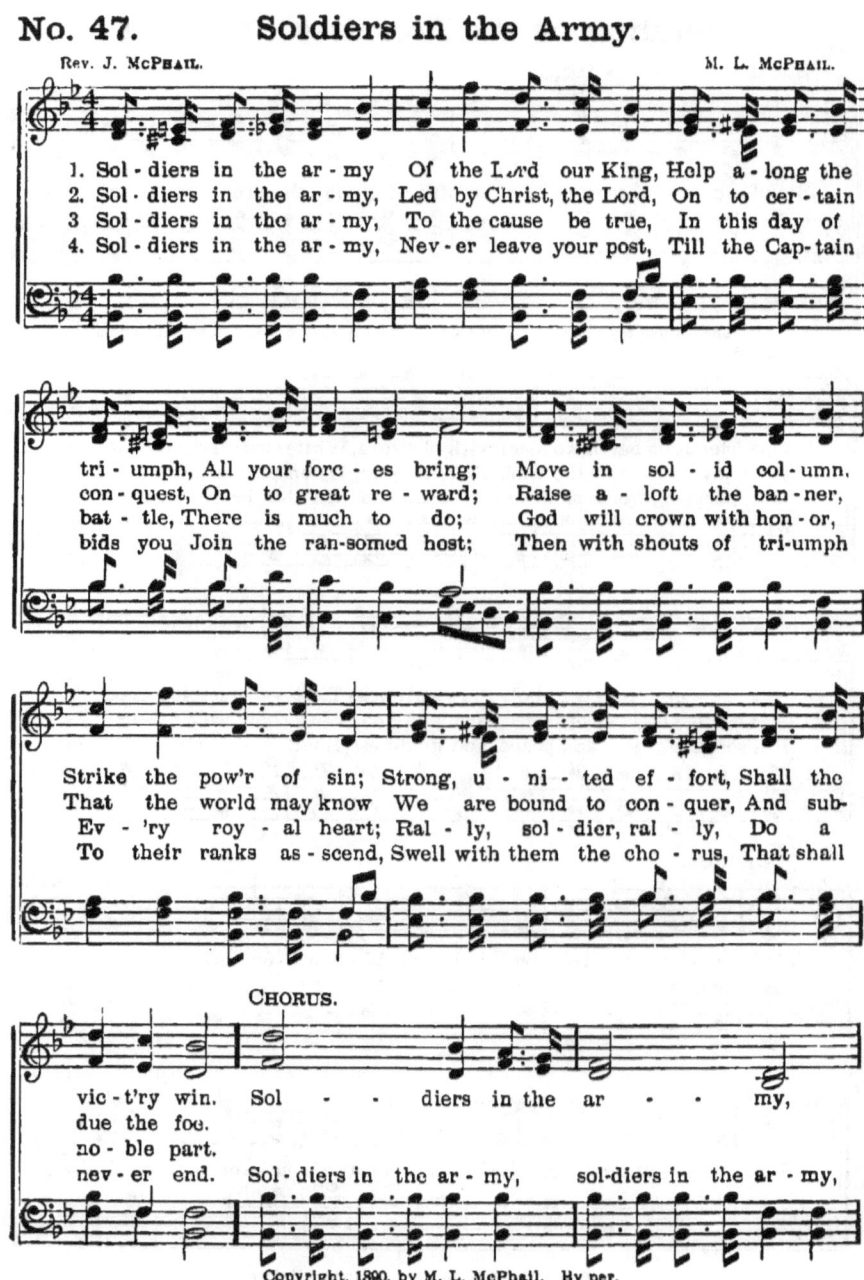

Soldiers in the Army. Concluded.

Strike with all your might, Strike with all your might; In the name of Je-sus, Strike, and put the foe to flight.
In the name of Je-sus, In the name of Je-sus, to flight.

Rit.

No. 48. My Country, 'tis of Thee.

S. F. SMITH.   AMERICA. 6s, 4s.

1. My country, 'tis of thee, Sweet land of lib-er-ty. Of thee I sing; Land where my
2. My na-tive country, thee, Land of the no-ble free, Thy name I love; I love thy
3. Let mu-sic swell the breeze, And ring from all the trees Sweet freedom's song; Let mortal
4. Our father's God, to Thee, Author of lib-er-ty, To Thee we sing; Long may our

Cres.

fathers died, Land of the Pilgrim's pride, From ev-'ry mountain side, Let freedom ring.
rocks and rills, Thy woods and templed hills, My heart with rapture thrills, Like that a-bove.
tongues awake, Let all that breathe partake, Let rocks their silence break, The sound prolong.
land be bright, With freedom's holy light, Protect us by Thy might, Great God, our King!

What a Gathering, etc.—Concluded.

The Best Friend is Jesus. Concluded.

CHORUS. *Spirited.*

The best friend to have is Je - - - - - sus, The best friend to have is
Je-sus ev-'ry day,

Je - - - - - sus, He will help you when you fall, He will
Je - sus all the way;

hear you when you call; Oh, the best friend to have is Je - sus.

No. 61. Behold! a Stranger.

JOSEPH GRIGG. H. K. OLIVER.

1. Be-hold a stran-ger's at the door! He gen-tly knocks, has knock'd be-fore:
2. But will He prove a friend in-deed? He will, the ver - y friend you need:
3. Oh, love-ly at - ti - tude!—He stands With melting heart and la - den hands;
4. Ad-mit Him, ere His an - ger burn; His feet de - part - ed, ne'er re-turn;

Has wait-ed long, is wait - ing still; You treat no oth - er friend so ill.
The man of Naz - a - reth—'tis He, With garments dyed at Cal - va - ry.
Oh, matchless kindness! and He shows This matchless kindness to His foes.
Ad - mit Him, or the hour's at hand When, at His door, de-nied you'll stand.

No. 68 "The Voice of the Holy Spirit Calls."

Sacred Song and Chorus.

Rev. Ford C. Ottman.   John B. Marsh.

1. The voice of the Holy Spirit calls Most won-drous-ly sweet and low;...... Up-on me the hush of e-ter-ni-ty falls, As He bids me a-rise and go..........
2. O shall I re-sist Thee, Heav'n-ly Dove, And cause Thee to plead in vain;...... Un-moved by Thy won-der-ful mes-sage of love Re-peat-ed a-gain and a-gain?..........
3. The Christ on Cal-v'ry died for me, Suff'ring my pain and woe;...... This the sweet mes-sage now whispered by Thee, As Thou bidst me a-rise and go..........
4. O Spir-it of Truth, with Thee for Guide, Since He hath lov'd me so;...... Lean-ing on Thee, as I walk by Thy side, To Je-sus, my Sav-ior, I'll go..........

Copyright, 1893, by P. P. Bilhorn.

"The Voice of the Holy Spirit Calls." Concluded.

CHORUS.
Go, child of the King - dom, Go in thy sor - row and sin;
Last v. Go, led by the Spir - it, Go in my sor - row and sin;
Go, child of the King - dom, Go in thy sor - row and sin;

Car - ry thy bur - den to Je - sus, Cast it all up - on Him.
Car - ry my bur - den to Je - sus, Cast it all up - on Him.
Car - ry thy bur - den to Je - sus, Cast it all up - on Him.

5 May I ever work for Thee;
 Thou hast given Thyself for me,
 Suff'ring on the cruel tree,
  All for me, Lord Jesus.

6 May Thy will be always mine.
 And my will be always Thine;
 Guided by Thy love divine,
  Live for Thee, Lord Jesus.

7 In my words and thoughts and ways
 May I always seek thy praise;
 Love and serve Thee all my days,
  Thee alone, Lord Jesus.

8 May I true and faithful be:
 Always strive to honor Thee;
 Then shall I Thy glory see;
  Dwell with Thee, Lord Jesus.

No. 75. Marching Onward.

Dr. M. H. Stephens.   P. P. Bilhorn.

1. "When you hear the sound of go-ing in the green tops of the trees,"
2. Ev-'ry-where there is an en-e-my, 'tis Sa-tan and his host;
3. To be read-y for the bat-tle we must keep our ar-mor on,
4. While we fight a-gainst the e-vil, let our hearts be filled with love,

Let us list-en to the word of God's com-mand (God's com-mand);
And Christ's message comes to-day with all its might (all its might)!
And the sword of God's own Spir-it in our hand (in our hand);
Then we'll point the vil-est sin-ner in the way (in the way),

Be ye read-y for the bat-tle, ev-er know-ing that God leads;
"Go ye there-fore in-to all the world," and bat-tle for the lost,
With the breast-plate of His right-eous-ness, the shield of faith so true,
That will lead them to the man-sion He's pre-par-ing them a-bove,

He will guide His sol-diers on-ward by His hand.
"And my Spir-it shall be with you" in the fight!
Let us trust Him, for He's a-ble to com-mand.
Where He'll meet us when we leave life's bat-tles' fray.

Copyright, 1893 by P. P. Bilhorn.

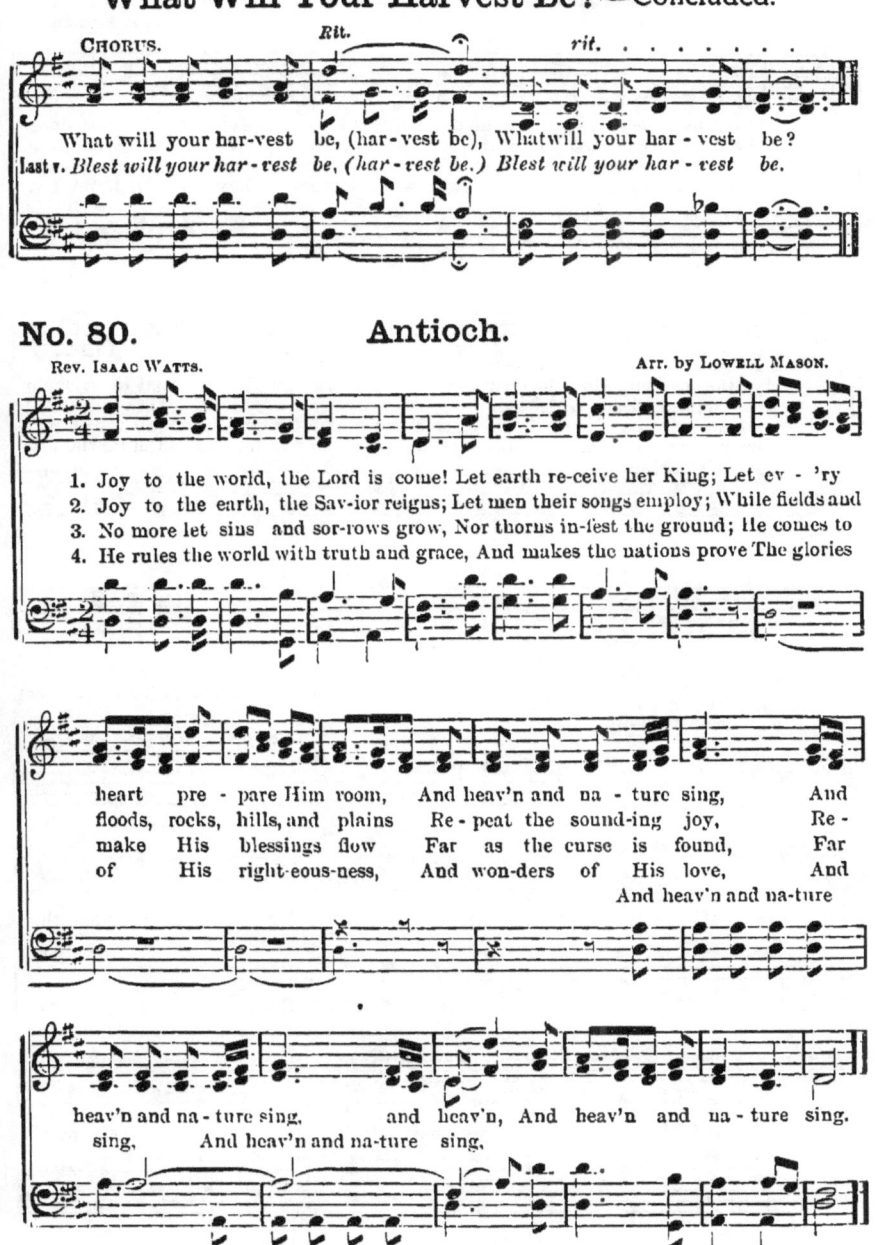

No. 84. "For the Lord God will Help Me."

Miss Eleanor W. Long.   Is. 50; 7.   P. P. Bilhorn.

1. Ev-'ry day, a-long life's path-way, Stretch-es out some cross for me, But I bear it, hop-ing, know-ing, As my days my strength shall be.
2. Ev-'ry day brings lit-tle du-ties, Ev-er-chang-ing, ev-er new, And the one that "li-eth near-est" Is the one that I shall do.
3. Tho' some sac-ri-fice must dai-ly Grace the al-tar of my heart, I will trust the hand that slays me— Noth-ing from His love can part.
4. So I plead His love and mer-cy, And His prom-is-es I claim, Tho' an host en-camp a-gainst me, I shall con-quer "In His name."

Chorus.

"For the Lord God will help me, There-fore shall I not be con-found-ed, There-fore have I set my face like a flint! And I know that I shall not be a-shamed."

Copyright, 1893, by P. P. Bilhorn.

My Name in Mother's Prayer.—Concluded.

In Sight of the Crystal Sea.—Concluded.

5 It seemed as tho' I woke from a dream,
 How sweet was the light of day!
Melodious sounded the Sabbath bells
 From towers that were far away;
I then became as a little child,
 And I wept and wept afresh;
For the Lord had taken my heart of stone,
 And given a heart of flesh.

6 Still oft I sit with life's memories,
 And I think of the crystal sea;   [ones,
And I see the thrones of the star-crown'd
 I know there's a crown for me; ["Come,"
And when the voice of the Judge says,
 Of the Judge on the great white throne,
I know 'mid the thrones of the star-crown'd
 There's one I shall call my own.   [ones,

No. 87.   Closer, Lord, to Thee.

"It is good for me to draw near to God."—Ps. 73: 28.

E. G. Taylor, D. D. Alt.   Geo. C. Stebbins.

1. Clos - er, Lord, to Thee I cling, Clos - er still to Thee;
2. Clos - er yet, O Lord, my Rock, Ref - uge of my soul;
3. Clos - er still, my Help, my Stay, Clos - er, clos - er still;
4. Clos - er, Lord, to Thee I come, Light of life di - vine;

Safe be - neath Thy shelter-ing wing I would ev - er be;
Dread I not the tem - pest-shock, Tho' the bil - lows roll.
Meek - ly there I learn to say, "Fa - ther, not my will;"
Thro' the ev - er bless - ed Son, Joy and peace are mine;

Rude the blast of doubt and sin, Fierce as - saults with-out, with - in,
Wild - est storm can - not a - larm, For to me can come no harm,
Learn that in af - flic - tion's hour, When the clouds of sor - row lower,
Let me in Thy love a - bide, Keep me ev - er by Thy side,

Help me, Lord, the bat - tle win;—Clos - er, Lord, to Thee.
Lean - ing on Thy lov - ing arm;—Clos - er, Lord, to Thee.
Love di - rects Thy band of power;—Clos - er, Lord, to Thee.
In the "Rock of A - ges" hide,—Clos - er, Lord, to Thee.

Copyright, 1882, by Geo. C. Stebbins. By per.

No. 90 — God be Merciful to Me.

Ps. 51.

P. B. P. BILHORN.

1. Lord, ac-cord-ing to Thy lov-ing kind-ness, Show Thy fa-vor un-to me;
2. Purge me thoroughly from all trans-gres-sions, Wash me whit-er than the snow;
3. Quick-en me ac-cord-ing to Thy judgments, Grant Thy mercies now to me;
4. I have longed, O Lord, for Thy sal-va-tion, And Thy law is my de-light;
5. Of-fer now un-to our God thanks-giv-ing, Pay thy vows to Him most high,

For the great-ness of Thy ten-der mer-cies, Blot out mine in-iq-ui-ty.
Teach me to observe Thy righteous judgments, Cause me in Thy paths to go.
Make Thy face to shine up-on Thy ser-vant, Let my soul now live in Thee.
Let my cry, O Lord, a-rise be-fore Thee, I will praise Thee day and night.
Call up-on Him, in thy heart re-pent-ing, With the brok-en heart-ed cry.

ff CHORUS. *p* *f*

God be mer-ci-ful to me, the sin-ner, God be mer-ci-ful to me;

Hear my pray'r O Lord, and save me, O God! be mer-ci-ful to me.

Copyright, 1891, by P. Bilhorn.

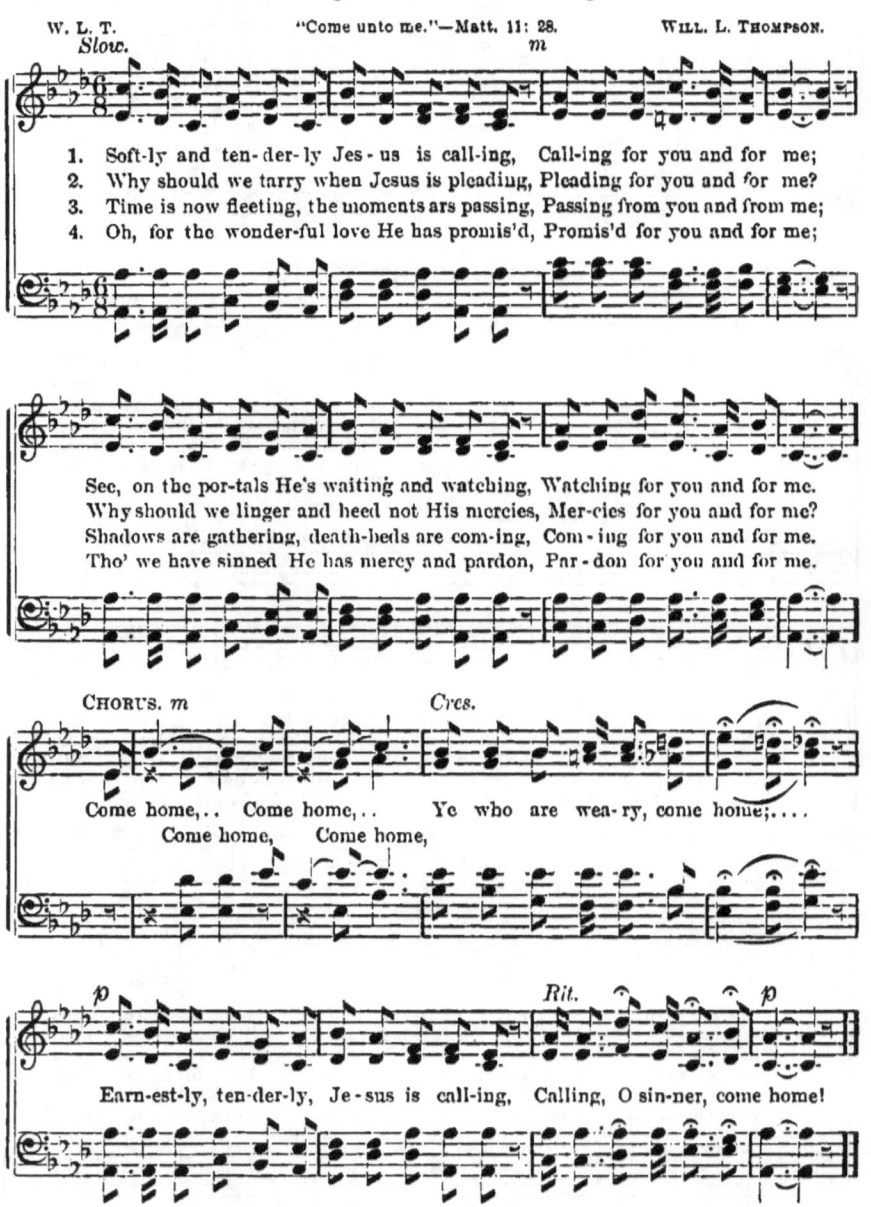

Steadily Marching On. Concluded.

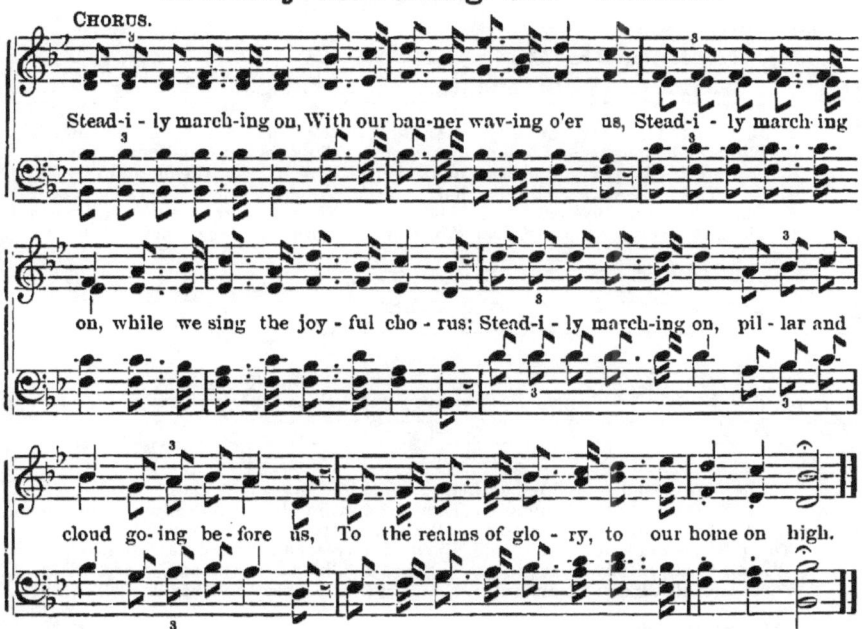

CHORUS.

Stead-i-ly march-ing on, With our ban-ner wav-ing o'er us, Stead-i-ly march-ing on, while we sing the joy-ful cho-rus; Stead-i-ly march-ing on, pil-lar and cloud go-ing be-fore us, To the realms of glo-ry, to our home on high.

No. 103 Art Thou Weary?

Tr. by T. M. NEALE. Rev. Sir HENRY BAKER.

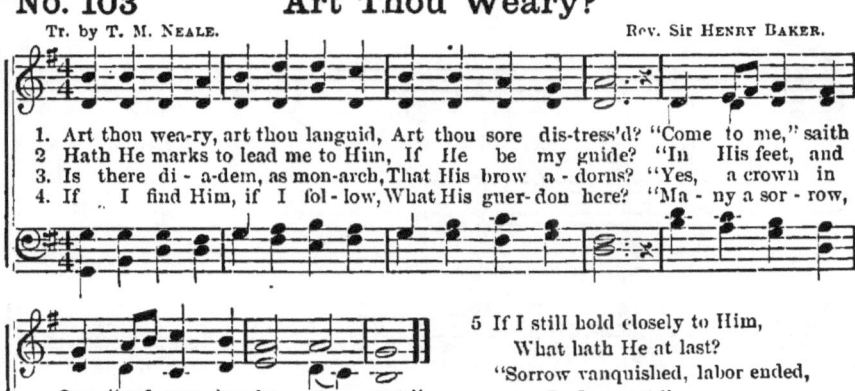

1. Art thou wea-ry, art thou languid, Art thou sore dis-tress'd? "Come to me," saith One, "and, com-ing, be at rest."
2. Hath He marks to lead me to Him, If He be my guide? "In His feet, and hands, are wound-prints, And His side."
3. Is there di-a-dem, as mon-arch, That His brow a-dorns? "Yes, a crown in ver-y sure-ty, But of thorns."
4. If I find Him, if I fol-low, What His guer-don here? "Ma-ny a sor-row, ma-ny a la-bor, Ma-ny a tear."

5 If I still hold closely to Him,
    What hath He at last?
   "Sorrow vanquished, labor ended,
    Jordan past."

6 If I ask Him to receive me,
    Will He say me nay?
   "Not till earth and not till heaven
    Pass away."

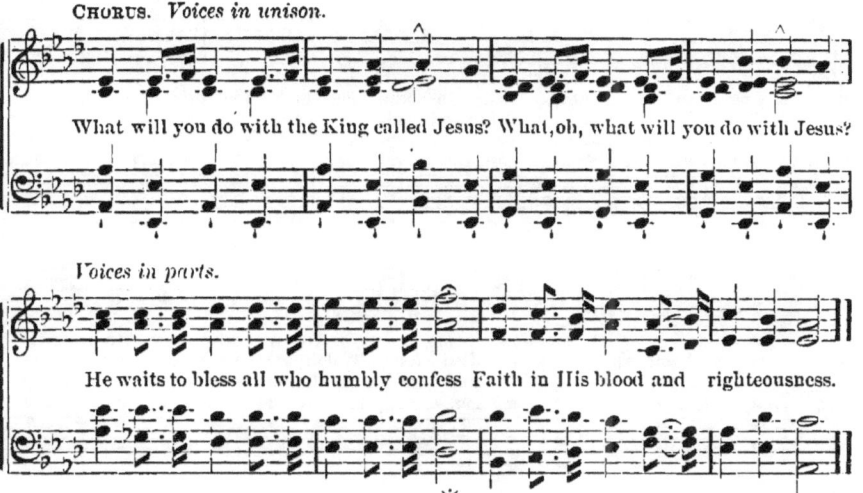

What will You Do? Concluded.

CHORUS. *Voices in unison.*

What will you do with the King called Jesus? What, oh, what will you do with Jesus?

Voices in parts.

He waits to bless all who humbly confess Faith in His blood and righteousness.

No. 109. There's a Wideness in God's Mercy.

FREDERICK W. FABER.   Ps. 136: 1–26.   LIZZIE S. TOURJEE.

1. There's a wide-ness in God's mer-cy, Like the wide-ness of the sea;
2. There is wel-come for the sin-ner, And more grac-es for the good;
3. For the love of God is broad-er Than the meas-ure of man's mind;
4. If our love were but more sim-ple, We should take Him at His word;

There's a kind-ness in His jus-tice, Which is more than lib-er-ty.
There is mer-cy with the Sav-ior; There is heal-ing in His blood.
And the heart of the E-ter-nal Is most won-der-ful-ly kind.
And our lives would be all sun-shine In the sweet-ness of our Lord.

Used by permission.

No. 114. All Taken Away.

R. Kelso Carter, (except 1st verse).   A. A.

1. Did you hear what Jesus said to me? They're all taken away, away;
   Your sins are pardoned and you are free, They're all taken away.
2. Oh, this wondrous grace so free and full; They're all taken away, away;
   Tho' red like crimson, they're now as wool; They're all taken away.
3. Now the cleansing streams of mercy flow; They're all taken away, away;
   My sins like scarlet are white as snow; They're all taken away.
4. I have plung'd beneath the crimson tide; They're all taken away, away;
   And now by faith I am purified; They're all taken away.

CHORUS.
They're all taken away, away, They're all taken away, away,
They're all taken away, away, My sins are all taken away.

5. Oh, the cleansing blood has washed my soul;
   They're all taken away, away;
   And Jesus' healing has made me whole;
   They're all taken away.
6. Now the Spirit witnesses to me;
   They're all taken away, away;
   And keeps me standing in liberty;
   They're all taken away.
7. So I praise the Lord for sins forgiven,
   They're all taken away, away;
   While onward pressing my way to heav'n;
   They're all taken away.
8. And when in glory we meet above;
   They're all taken away, away;
   We'll sing the song of Redeeming Love;
   They're all taken away.

Copyright, 1891, by R. Kelso Carter. Used by permission.

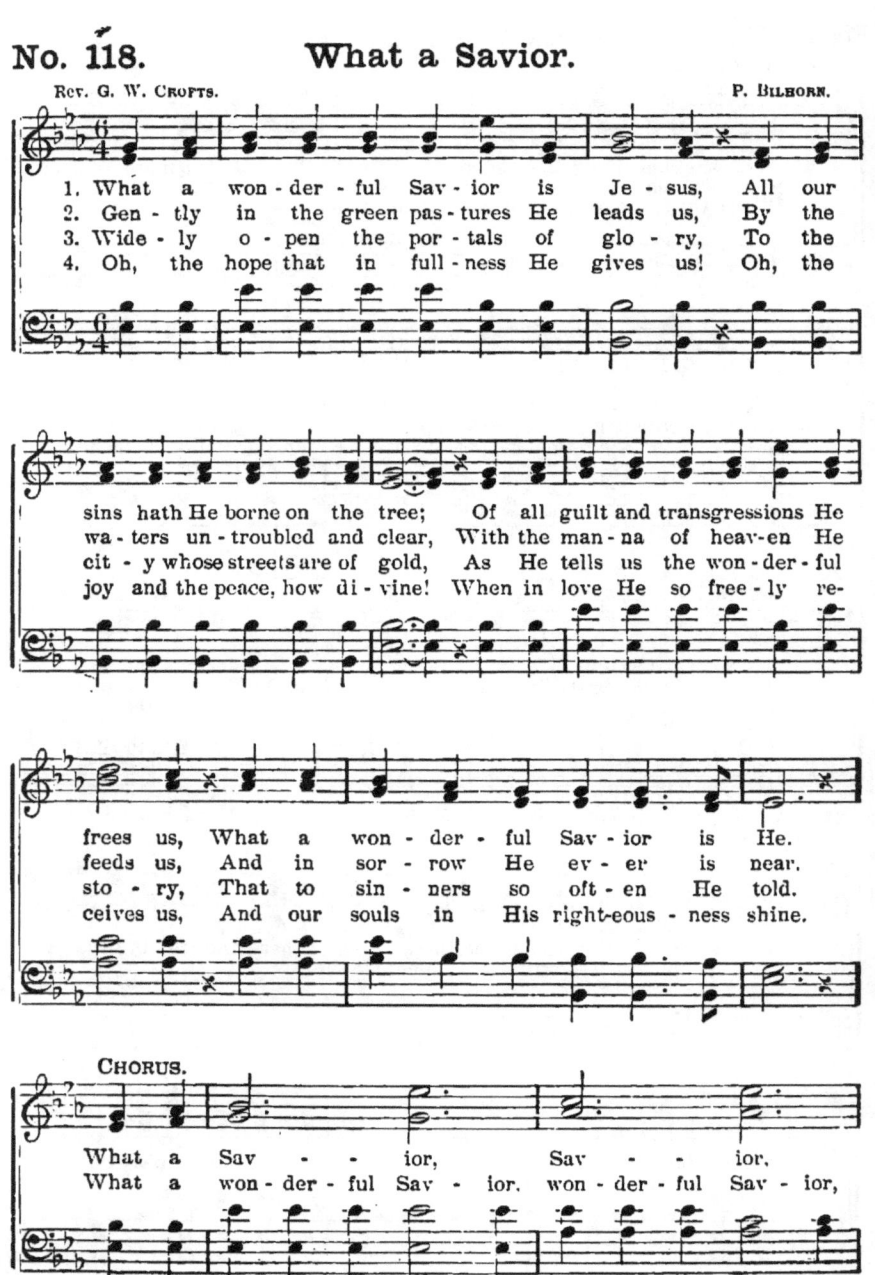

What a Savior. Concluded.

No. 119. Holy Spirit, Faithful Guide.

M. M. W.
M. M. Wells.

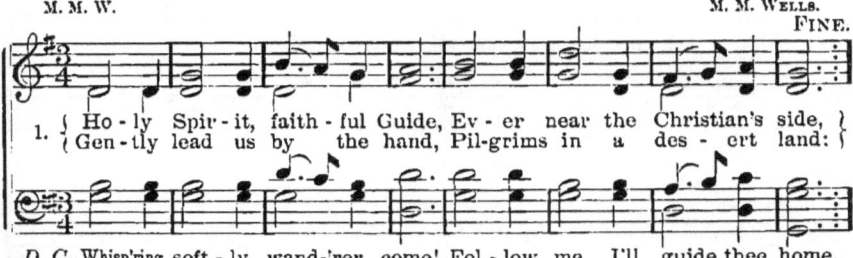

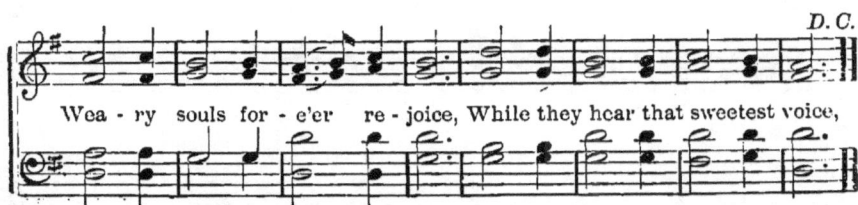

2 Ever present, truest Friend,
  Ever near, Thine aid to lend,
  Leave us not to doubt and fear,
  Groping on in darkness drear.
  When the storms are raging sore,
  Hearts grow faint, and hopes give o'er;
  Whisper softly, wand'rer, come!
  Follow me, I'll guide thee home.

3 When our days of toil shall cease,
  Waiting still for sweet release,
  Nothing left but heaven and prayer,
  Wond'ring if our names are there;
  Wading deep the dismal flood,
  Pleading naught but Jesus' blood;
  Whisper softly, wand'rer, come!
  Follow me, I'll guide thee home.

No. 120. His Yoke is Easy.

"The Lord is my shepherd; I shall not want. He maketh me to lie down in green pastures: he leadeth me beside the still waters. He restoreth my soul: he leadeth me in the paths of righteousness for his name's sake. Yea, though I walk through the valley of the shadow of death, I will fear no evil: for thou art with me; thy rod and thy staff they comfort me. Thou preparest a table before me in the presence of mine enemies: thou anointest my head with oil: my cup runneth over. Surely goodness and mercy shall follow me all the days of my life: and I will dwell in the house of the Lord forever."—Psa. 23.

R. E. HUDSON.

1. The Lord is my Shep-herd, I shall not want, He mak-eth me down to lie In pas-ture green, He lead-eth me The qui-et wa-ters by.
2. My soul cri-eth out: "Re-store me a-gain, And give me the strength to take The nar-row path of right-eous-ness, E'en for His own name's sake."
3. Yea, tho' I should walk in the valley of death, Yet why should I fear from ill? For Thou art with me, and Thy rod And staff com-fort me still.

CHORUS.

His yoke is eas-y, His bur-den is light, I've found it so, I've found it so; He lead-eth me by day and by night, Where liv-ing wa-ters flow.

Copyright, 1886, by R. E. Hudson. By per.

No. 121. What Will You Do?

Arr. by P. P. B.
J. Wilbur Chapman. D. D.

1. Oh, what will you do in the sol-emn day, When heav'n and earth shall pass a-way; When the sun shall be dark the moon give no light! The stars of heav-en shall take their flight?
2. Oh, what will you do when your sins at last Shall rise like clouds that gath-er fast, And shall stand be-fore you in dread ar-ray; O sin-ner, tell me, what will you say?
3. Oh, what will you do when this life is past, The door of mer-cy closed at last; When all hope shall have fled, the last chance gone, And you must stand be-fore God a-lone?
4. Then which shall it be, will you still de-lay, Or will you trust in Christ to-day? 'Tis the voice of God's love now calls to thee, Oh, where will you spend E-ter-ni-ty?

CHORUS.

What will you do?......... What will you do?
What will you do?......... What will you do In the sol-emn day?

Rit. - - -

Copyright, 1894, by P. P. Bilhorn.

Jesus Saves Me To-day. Concluded.

That He came from a-bove, Je-sus saves and He keeps me to-day.

No. 127. Heaven is not Far Away.

C. F. L.   C. E. LESLIE. By per.

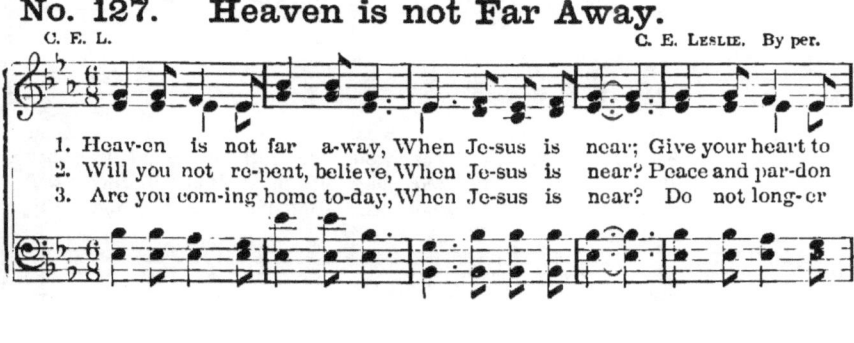

1. Heav-en is not far a-way, When Je-sus is near; Give your heart to
2. Will you not re-pent, believe, When Je-sus is near? Peace and par-don
3. Are you com-ing home to-day, When Je-sus is near? Do not long-er

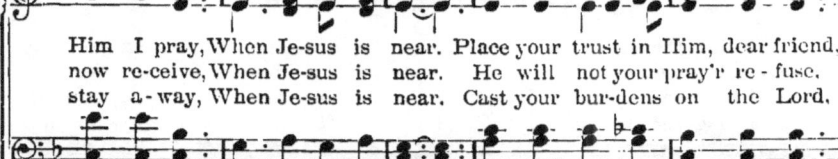

Him I pray, When Je-sus is near. Place your trust in Him, dear friend,
now re-ceive, When Je-sus is near. He will not your pray'r re-fuse,
stay a-way, When Je-sus is near. Cast your bur-dens on the Lord,

Rit. - - - -

He will keep you to the end, Heav-en is not far a-way, When Jesus is near.
Come and now the Savior choose, Heav-en is not far a-way, When Jesus is near.
He has prom-ised in His word, Heav-en is not far a-way, When Jesus is near.

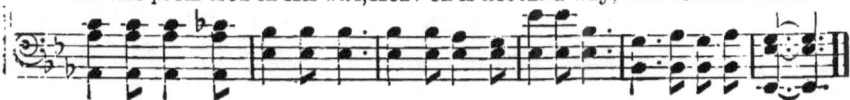

Copyright by C. E. Leslie.

No. 128. Seeking for Me.

"For the Son of Man is come to seek and save that which was lost."—Luke 19: 10.

E. E. Hasty. By per.

1. Je-sus, my Sav-ior, to Beth-le-hem came, Born in a man-ger to sor-row and shame; Oh! it was won-der-ful! blest be His name!
2. Je-sus, my Sav-ior, on Cal-va-ry's tree, Paid the great debt, and my soul He set free; Oh! it was won-der-ful! how could it be?
3. Je-sus, my Sav-ior, the same as of old, While I did wan-der a-far from the fold, Gen-tly and long He hath plead with my soul,
4. Je-sus, my Sav-ior, shall come from on high, Sweet is the prom-ise as wea-ry years fly; Oh! I shall see Him de-scend-ing the sky,

Refrain.

Seek-ing for me, for me, Seek-ing for me, Seek-ing for me, Seek-ing for me, Seek-ing for me, Oh! it was won-der-ful!
Dy-ing for me, for me, Dy-ing for me, Dy-ing for me, Dy-ing for me, Dy-ing for me, Oh! it was won-der-ful!
Call-ing for me, for me, Call-ing for me, Call-ing for me, Call-ing for me, Call-ing for me, Gen-tly and long He hath
Com-ing for me, for me, Com-ing for me, Com-ing for me, Com-ing for me, Com-ing for me, Oh, I shall see Him de-

They Sing a New Song. Concluded.

No. 141. Take my Life and let it Be.

FRANCES R. HAVERGALL.   HENDON.   C. H. A. MALAN.

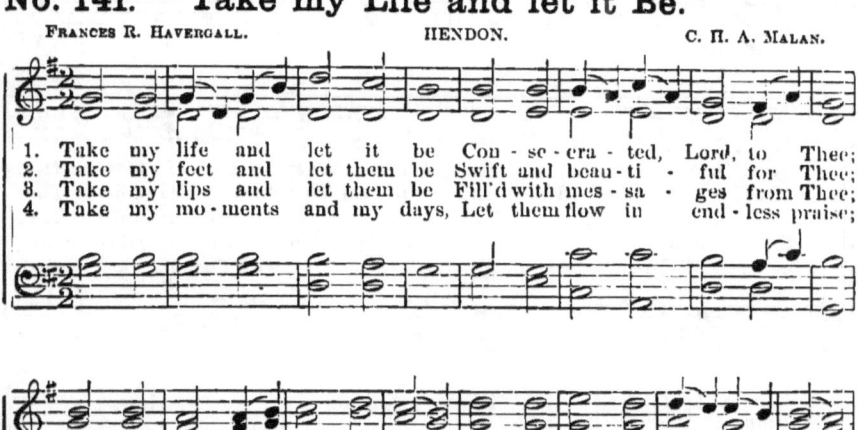

1. Take my life and let it be Con-se-cra-ted, Lord, to Thee;
2. Take my feet and let them be Swift and beau-ti-ful for Thee;
3. Take my lips and let them be Fill'd with mes-sa-ges from Thee;
4. Take my mo-ments and my days, Let them flow in end-less praise;

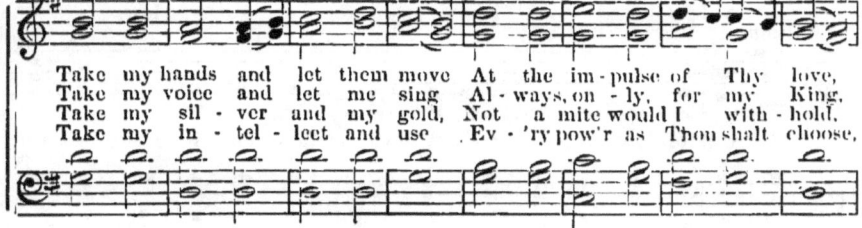

Take my hands and let them move At the im-pulse of Thy love,
Take my voice and let me sing Al-ways, on-ly, for my King,
Take my sil-ver and my gold, Not a mite would I with-hold,
Take my in-tel-lect and use Ev-'ry pow'r as Thou shalt choose,

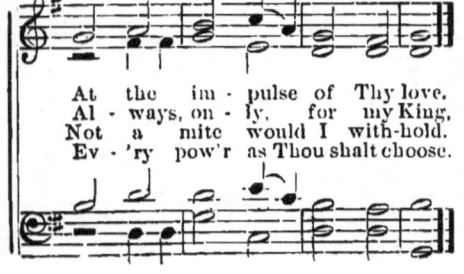

At the im-pulse of Thy love.
Al-ways, on-ly, for my King,
Not a mite would I with-hold.
Ev-'ry pow'r as Thou shalt choose.

5 Take my will and make it thine,
It shall be no longer mine;
Take my heart, it is Thine own,
It shall be Thy royal Throne.

6 Take my love, my God, I pour
At Thy feet its treasure-store;
Take myself, and I will be
Ever, only, all for Thee.

The Palace of the King. Concluded.

3 She cometh to the King
  In robes with needle wrought;
The virgins that do follow her
  Shall unto Thee be brought.
With gladness and with joy,
  Thou all of them shalt bring,
And they together enter shall
  The palace of the King.
    Cho.—With gladness, etc.

4 And in Thy father's stead,
  Thy children thou shalt take,
And in all places of the earth
  Them noble princes make.
I will show forth thy name
  To generations all;
The people therefore evermore
  To Thee give praises shall.
    Cho.—With gladness, etc.

No. 145. Oh, Happy Day.

"Happy is that people whose God is the Lord."—Psa. 144: 15.

P. DODDRIDGE.   E. F. RIMBAULT.

1. Oh, hap-py day, that fixed my choice, On Thee my Sav-iour, and my God!
   Well may this glow-ing heart re-joice, And tell its rapt-ures all a-broad.

CHORUS.   FINE.

Hap-py day, hap-py day, When Je-sus washed my sins a-way,

D.S.

He taught me how to watch and pray, And live re-joic-ing ev-'ry day.

2 'Tis done, the great transaction's done;
  I am the Lord's and He is mine;
He drew me and I follow'd on,
  Charmed to confess the voice divine.

3 Now rest, my long-divided heart!
  Fixed on this blissful center, rest;
Nor ever from thy Lord depart,
  With Him, of every good possessed.

No. 149. Holy, Holy! Lord God Almighty!

REGINALD HEBER, D. D. Rev. 4: 6. REV. JOHN B. DYKES.

1. Ho-ly, Ho-ly, Ho-ly! Lord God Al-migh-ty!
2. Ho-ly, Ho-ly, Ho-ly! all the saints a-dore Thee,
3. Ho-ly, Ho-ly, Ho-ly! tho' the dark-ness hide Thee,
4. Ho-ly, Ho-ly, Ho-ly! Lord God Al-migh-ty!

Ear-ly in the morn-ing our song shall rise to Thee;
Cast-ing down their gold-en crowns a-round the glass-y sea;
Though the eye of sin-ful man Thy glo-ry may not see,
All Thy works shall praise Thy name in earth, and sky, and sea;

Ho-ly, Ho-ly, Ho-ly! Mer-ci-ful and Migh-ty!
Cher-u-bim and Ser-a-phim fall-ing down be-fore Thee;
On-ly Thou art Ho-ly, there is none be-side Thee,
Ho-ly, Ho-ly, Ho-ly! Mer-ci-ful and Migh-ty!

God in three Per-sons, bless-ed Trin-i-ty!
Which wert and art, and ev-er-more shalt be.
Per-fect in pow'r, in love, and pu-ri-ty.
God in three Per-sons, bless-ed Trin-i-ty! A-men.

Waiting for the Savior. Concluded.

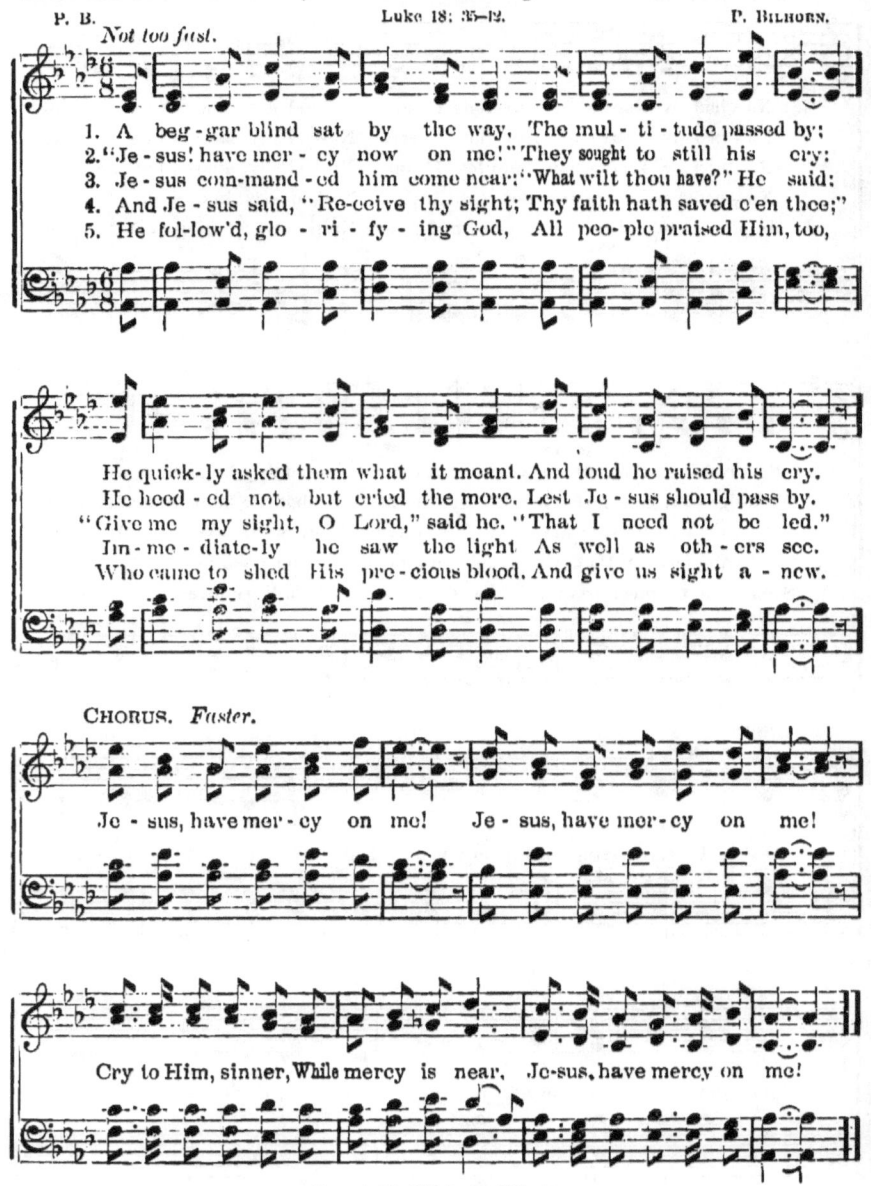

Ready and Willing to Save. Concluded.

Je-sus is will-ing, Je-sus is read-y and will-ing to save.

No. 159. O Day of Rest and Gladness.

C. WORDSWORTH.   German Melody.

1. O day of rest and glad-ness, O day of joy and light;
   O balm of care and sad-ness, Most beau-ti-ful, most bright;
2. On thee, at the cre-a-tion, The light first had its birth;
   On thee, for our sal-va-tion, Christ rose from depths of earth;
3. New grac-es ev-er gain-ing From this our day of rest,
   We reach the rest re-main-ing To spir-its of the blest;

On thee the high and low-ly, Thro' a-ges joined in tune,
On thee, our Lord vic-to-rious, The Spir-it sent from heav'n;
To Ho-ly Ghost be prais-es, To Fa-ther, and to Son;

Sing "Ho-ly, ho-ly, ho-ly," To the great God Tri-une.
And thus on thee, most glo-rious, A tri-ple light was giv'n.
The Church her voice up-rais-es To Thee, blest Three in One.

"Wilt Thou be Made Whole?"—Concluded.

No. 163. Martyn.

C. WESLEY. S. B. MARSH.

1. Sin-ners, turn, why will ye die? God, your Mak-er, asks you—Why?
   God, who did your be-ing give, Made you with Him-self to live;
   He the fa-tal cause de-mands, Asks the work of His own hands.—
   D.C.—Why, ye thank-less crea-tures, why Will ye cross His love, and die?

2 Sinners, turn, why will ye die?
God, your Savior, asks you—Why?
He who did your souls retrieve,
Died Himself that ye might live;
Will you let Him die in vain?
Crucify your Lord again?
Why, ye ransomed sinners, why
Will ye slight His grace, and die?

3 Sinners, turn, why will ye die?
God, the Spirit, asks you—Why?
He, who all your lives hath strove,
Urged you to embrace His love;
Will ye not His grace receive?
Will ye still refuse to live?
Why, ye long-sought sinners, why
Will ye grieve your God, and die?

Farewell. Concluded.

I'll bid you farewell, I'll bid you farewell, We scarce know our friends till we bid them farewell.
I'll bid you farewell, I'll bid you farewell, They take on life's verge an e-ter-nal fare-well.
I'll bid you farewell, I'll bid you farewell, Till judgment day breaketh I bid you farewell.

No. 167. Mercy's Free.

R. JUKES. From D. F. E. AUBER.

1. By faith I view my Sav-ior dy-ing, On the tree, On the tree;
   To ev-'ry na-tion He is cry-ing, Look to me, Look to me;
2. Did Christ, when I was sin pur-su-ing, Pit-y me, Pit-y me?
   And did He snatch my soul from sin? Can it be, Can it be?

He bids the guilt-y now draw near, Re-pent, be-lieve, dismiss their fear;
Oh, yes! He did sal-va-tion bring; He is my Prophet, Priest, and King;

Hark, hark, what precious words I hear, Mer-cy's free, Mer-cy's free.
And now my hap-py soul can sing, Mer-cy's free, Mer-cy's free.

3 Jesus my weary soul refreshes:
  Mercy's free, Mercy's free,
 And every moment Christ is precious
  Unto me, Unto me;
 None can describe the bliss I prove,
 While through this wilderness I rove,
 All may enjoy the Savior's love,
  Mercy's free, Mercy's free.

4 Long as I live, I'll still be crying,
  Mercy's free, Mercy's free,
 And this shall be my theme when dying,
  Mercy's free, Mercy's free,
 And when the vale of death I've passed,
 When lodged above the stormy blast,
 I'll sing, while endless ages last,
  Mercy's free, Mercy's free.

Seeking the Lost.—Concluded.

In - to the fold of my Re-deem - er,
In - to the fold............ of my Redeem - er,...... Je - sus the
Je - sus, the Lamb for sin - ners slain, for sin - ners slain.
Lamb,................ for sin - ners slain................

No. 169. Oh, For a Heart.

Scottish Tune.

1. Oh, for a heart to praise my God, A heart from sin set free!
2. A heart re-signed, sub - miss-ive, meek, My great Re - deem-er's throne;

A heart that al-ways feels Thy blood, So free - ly spilt for me!
Where on - ly Christ is heard to speak; Where Je - sus reigns a - lone.

3 Oh, for a lowly, contrite heart,
   Believing, true, and clean,
  Which neither life nor death can part
   From Him that dwells within!

4 A heart in every thought renewed,
   And full of love divine;
  Perfect and right, and pure and good,
   A copy, Lord, of Thine.

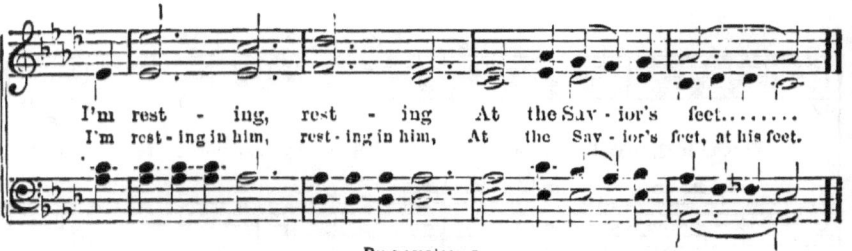

The Penitent's Plea. Concluded.

CHORUS. *mp*

once more? / ing heart. / ing soul. Grace there is my ev'-ry debt to pay,

Cres.
Blood to wash my ev-'ry sin a-way, Pow'r to

Dim.
keep me sinless day by day, For me, for me!

No. 175. My Soul, be on Thy Guard.

GEORGE HEATH.   Dr. LOWELL MASON.

1. My soul, be on thy guard; Ten thou-sand foes a-rise;
2. Oh, watch, and fight, and pray; The bat-tle ne'er give o'er;
3. Ne'er think the vic-t'ry won, Nor lay thine ar-mor down;

The hosts of sin are press-ing hard To draw thee from the skies.
Re-new it bold-ly ev-'ry day, And help di-vine im-plore.
The work of faith will not be done, Till thou ob-tain the crown.

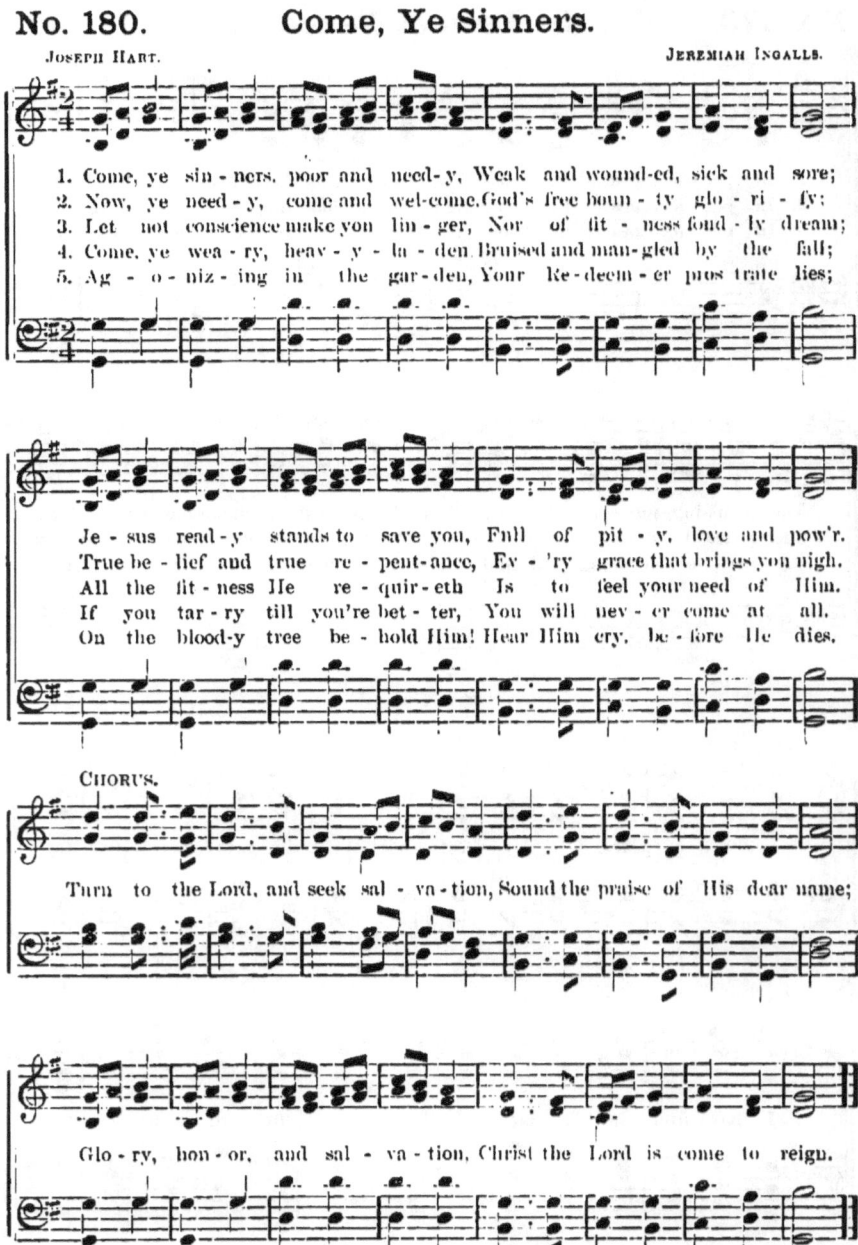

Is There One Prepared? Concluded.

will............	those man - sions	see,.............. Is there
will............	those bright crowns	be,..............
have...........	them, they are	free,.............
sweet..........	this sound will	be,.............

one............... pre - pared for me?

No. 183. Hamburg. L. M.

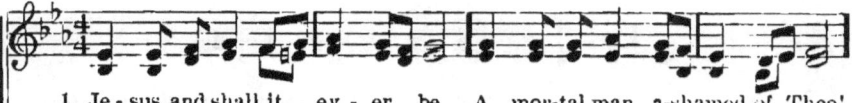

1. Je - sus, and shall it ev - er be, A mor-tal man a-shamed of Thee!
2. A-shamed of Je - sus! that dear Friend On whom my hopes of heav'n de-pend!

A-shamed of Thee whom an-gels praise, Whose glories shine thro' endless days!
No, when I blush, be this my shame—That I no more re-vere His name.

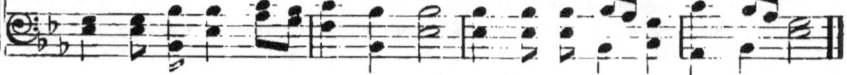

3 Ashamed of Jesus! yes I may,
When I've no guilt to wash away;
No tear to wipe, no good to crave,
No fears to quell, no soul to save.

4 Till then—nor is my boasting vain—
Till then, I boast a Savior slain:
And oh, may this my glory be—
That Christ is not ashamed of me.

Master, the Tempest is Raging. Concluded.

No. 190. Blest be the Tie.
Rev. John Fawcett. — DENNIS. — From H. G. Nageli.

No. 191. Come, Thou Fount.
Rev. R. Robinson, 1758. — NETTLETON. — Old Melody, 1812.

2 Here I'll raise my Ebenezer,
  Hither by Thy help I'm come;
And I hope by Thy good pleasure,
  Safely to arrive at home.
Jesus sought me when a stranger,
  Wandering from the fold of God;
He to rescue me from danger
  Interposed His precious blood.

3 Oh, to grace how great a debtor,
  Daily I'm constrained to be!
Let Thy goodness as a fetter,
  Bind my wandering heart to Thee;
Prone to wander, Lord, I feel it—
  Prone to leave the God I love—
Here's my heart, oh, take and seal it,
  Seal it for Thy courts above.

No. 192. What a Friend.

H. BONAR.   C. C. CONVERSE, By per.

1. What a friend we have in Jesus, All our sins and griefs to bear!
What a privilege to carry Ev'rything to God in prayer!
D.S. All because we do not carry Ev'rything to God in prayer!

Oh, what peace we often forfeit, Oh, what needless pain we bear,

2 Have we trials and temptations?
Is there trouble anywhere?
We should never be discouraged,
Take it to the Lord in prayer.
Can we find a friend so faithful,
Who will all our sorrows share?
Jesus knows our every weakness,
Take it to the Lord in prayer.

3 Are we weak and heavy laden,
Cumbered with a load of care?
Precious Saviour, still our refuge,—
Take it to the Lord in prayer.
Do thy friends despise, forsake thee?
Take it to the Lord in prayer;
In His arms He'll take and shield thee.
Thou wilt find a solace there.

No. 193. Rock of Ages.

A. M. TOPLADY.   THOS. HASTINGS.

1. Rock of Ages cleft for me, Let me hide myself in Thee;
D.C. Be of sin the double cure, Save from wrath and make me pure.

{ Let the water and the blood,
  From Thy wounded side which flow'd, }

2 Could my tears forever flow,
Could my zeal no languor know,
These for sin could not atone;
Thou must save, and Thou alone
In my hand no price I bring;
Simply to thy cross I cling.
3 While I draw this fleeting breath,
When my eyes shall close in death,
When I rise to worlds unknown,
And behold Thee on Thy Throne,
Rock of Ages cleft for me,
Let me hide myself in Thee,

No. 194. Cross and Crown.

THOMAS SHEPHERD.   GEO. N. ALLEN.

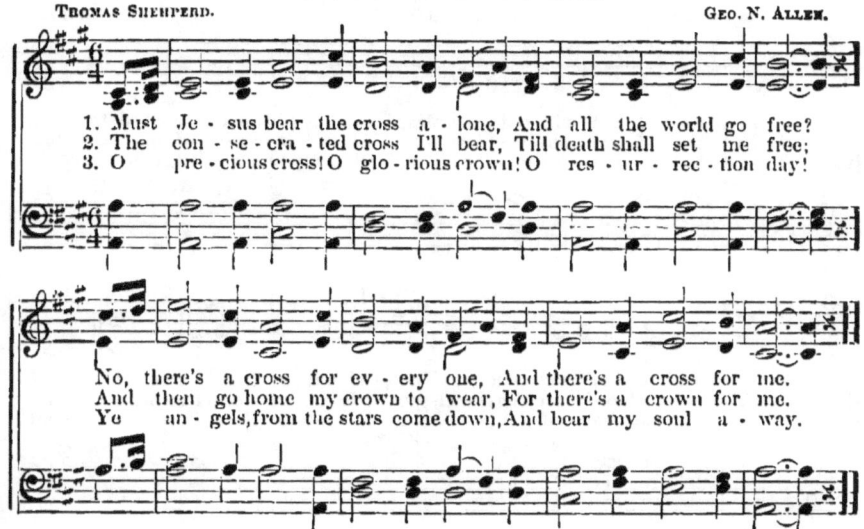

1. Must Jesus bear the cross alone, And all the world go free? No, there's a cross for every one, And there's a cross for me.
2. The consecrated cross I'll bear, Till death shall set me free; And then go home my crown to wear, For there's a crown for me.
3. O precious cross! O glorious crown! O resurrection day! Ye angels, from the stars come down, And bear my soul away.

No. 195. Jesus, Lover of My Soul.

CHARLES WESLEY.   MARTYN 7s, D.   S. B. MARSH.

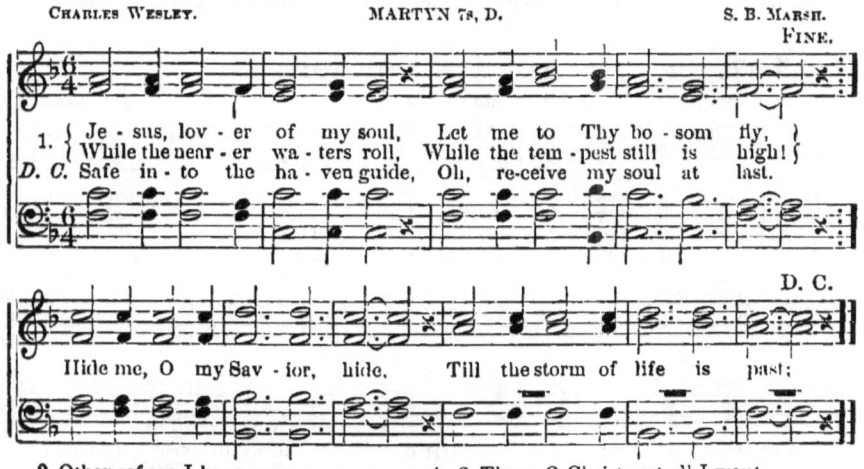

1. Jesus, lover of my soul, Let me to Thy bosom fly,
While the nearer waters roll, While the tempest still is high!
D.C. Safe into the haven guide, Oh, receive my soul at last.

Hide me, O my Savior, hide. Till the storm of life is past;

2 Other refuge I have none,
  Hangs my helpless soul on Thee;
Leave, oh leave me not alone,
  Still support and comfort me.
All my trust on Thee is stayed,
  All my help from Thee I bring;
Cover my defenceless head
  With the shadow of Thy wing.

3 Thou, O Christ, art all I want;
  More than all in Thee I find;
Raise the fallen! cheer the faint!
  Heal the sick! and lead the blind!
Just and holy is Thy Name,
  I am all unrighteousness:
Vile and full of sin I am,
  Thou art full of truth and **grace.**

No. 196. Just as I Am.

CHALOTTE ELLIOTT. WOODWORTH. L. M. WM. B. BRADBURY.

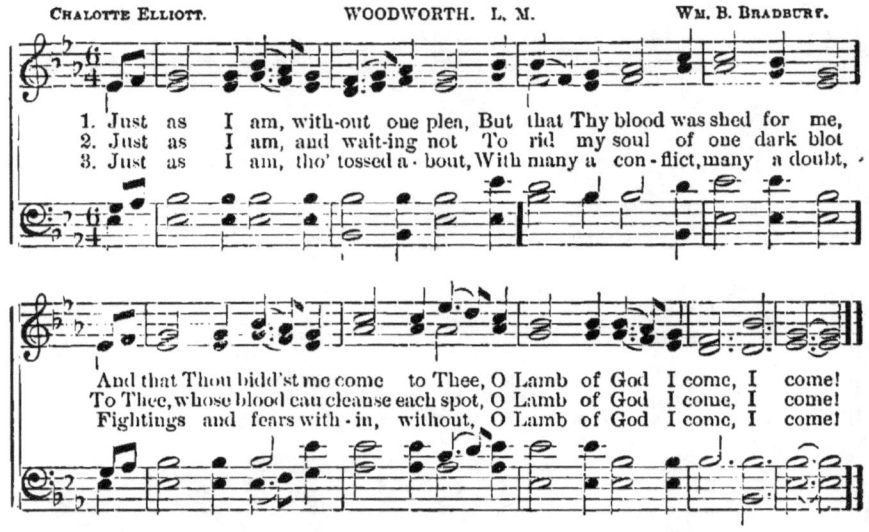

1. Just as I am, with-out one plea, But that Thy blood was shed for me,
2. Just as I am, and wait-ing not To rid my soul of one dark blot
3. Just as I am, tho' tossed a-bout, With many a con-flict, many a doubt,

And that Thou bidd'st me come to Thee, O Lamb of God I come, I come!
To Thee, whose blood can cleanse each spot, O Lamb of God I come, I come!
Fightings and fears with-in, without, O Lamb of God I come, I come!

4 Just as I am, poor, wretched, blind,
Sight, riches, healing of the mind,
Yea, all I need in Thee to find,
O Lamb of God! I come, I come!

5 Just as I am; Thou wilt receive,
Wilt welcome, pardon, cleanse, relieve;
Because Thy promise I believe,
O Lamb of God! I come, I come!

No. 197. Am I a Soldier.

ISAAC WATTS. ARLINGTON. C. M. THOS. A. ARNE.

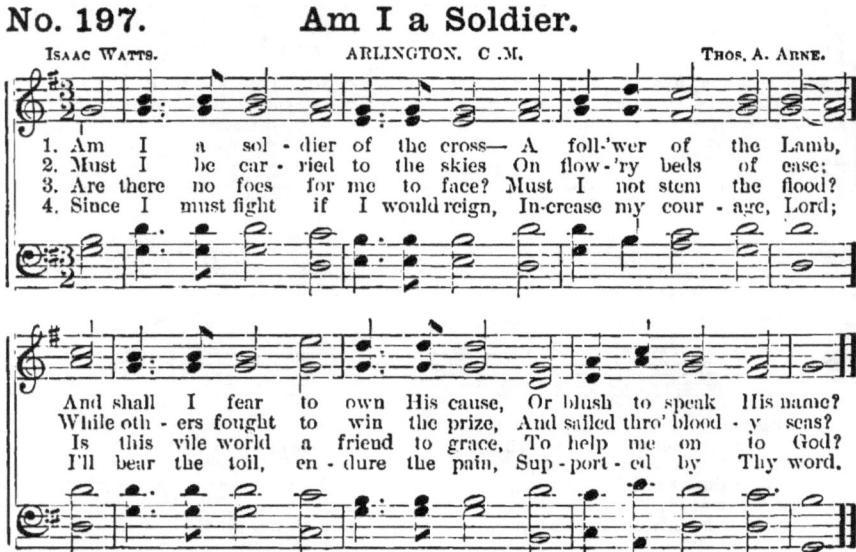

1. Am I a sol-dier of the cross— A foll-'wer of the Lamb,
2. Must I be car-ried to the skies On flow-'ry beds of ease;
3. Are there no foes for me to face? Must I not stem the flood?
4. Since I must fight if I would reign, In-crease my cour-age, Lord;

And shall I fear to own His cause, Or blush to speak His name?
While oth-ers fought to win the prize, And sailed thro' blood-y seas?
Is this vile world a friend to grace, To help me on to God?
I'll bear the toil, en-dure the pain, Sup-port-ed by Thy word.

No. 198. Nearer, My God, to Thee.

1 Nearer, my God, to Thee;
    Nearer to Thee;
  E'en though it be a cross,
    That raiseth me,
  Still all my song shall be,
  |:Nearer, my God, to thee,:|
    Nearer to Thee,

2 Though like the wanderer,
    The sun gone down,
  Darkness be over me,
    My rest a stone,
  Yet in my dreams I'd be
  |:Nearer, my God, to thee,:|
    Nearer to Thee.

3 There let the way appear,
    Steps unto heaven;
  All that Thou sendest me,
    In mercy given;
  Angels to beckon me
  |:Nearer, my God, to Thee,:|
    Nearer to thee.

No. 199. Work, for the Night is Coming.

1 Work, for the night is coming,
    Work, through the morning hours;
  Work, while the dew is sparkling,
    Work, 'mid springing flowers;
  Work, when the day grows brighter,
    Work in the glowing sun;
  Work, for the night is coming,
    When man's work is done.

2 Work, for the night is coming,
    Work through the sunny noon;
  Fill brightest hours with labor,
    Rest comes sure and soon,
  Give every flying minute,
    Something to keep in store;
  Work, for the night is coming,
    When man works no more.

3 Work, for the night is coming,
    Under the sunset skies;
  While the bright tints are glowing,
    Work, for the daylight flies,
  Work till the last beam fadeth,
    Fadeth to shine no more;
  Work while the night is darkening,
    When man's work is o'er.

No. 200. There is a Fountain

1 There is a fountain filled with blood,
    Drawn from Immanuel's veins;
  And sinners plunged beneath that flood,
    Lose all their guilty stains.

2 The dying thief rejoiced to see
    That fountain in his day;
  And there may I though vile as he,
    Wash all my sins away.

3 Then in a nobler, sweet song,
    I'll sing Thy power to save,
  When this poor lisping, stammering tongue
    Lies silent in the grave.

No. 201. I Hear the Savior Say

1 I hear the Savior say,
    Thy strength indeed is small;
  Child of weakness, watch and pray,
    Find in Me thine all in all.

Cho.—Jesus paid it all,
    All to Him I owe;
  Sin had left a crimson stain:
    He washed it white as snow.

2 Lord, now indeed I find
    Thy pow'r, and that alone,
  Can change the leper's spots,
    And melt the heart of stone.—Cho.

3 For nothing good have I
    Whereby Thy grace to claim—
  I'll wash my garments white
    In the blood of Calvary's Lamb.—Cho.

4 And when before the throne
    I stand in Him complete,
  I'll lay my trophies down,
    All down at Jesus' feet.—Cho.

No. 202 I Hear Thy Welcome Voice.

1 I hear Thy welcome voice,
    That calls me, Lord, to Thee,
  For cleansing in Thy precious blood,
    That flowed on Calvary.

Cho.—I am coming, Lord,
    Coming now to Thee!
  Wash me, cleanse me in the blood,
    That flowed on Calvary.

2 Though coming weak and vile,
    Thou dost my strength assure;
  Thou dost my vileness fully cleanse,
    Till spotless all and pure.

No. 203. All Hail the Power.

1 All hail the power of Jesus' name!
　Let angels prostrate fall;
　Bring forth the royal diadem,
　And crown Him Lord of all.

2 Crown Him, ye morning stars of light,
　Who fixed this earthly ball;
　Now hail the strength of Israel's might,
　And crown Him Lord of all.

3 Ye chosen seed of Israel's race,
　Ye ransomed from the fall,
　Hail Him who saves you by His grace,
　And crown Him Lord of all.

4 Sinners, whose love can ne'er forget
　The wormwood and the gall;
　Go, spread your trophies at His feet,
　And crown Him Lord of all.

5 Let every kindred, every tribe,
　On this terrestrial ball,
　To Him all majesty ascribe,
　And crown Him Lord of all.

6 O that with yonder sacred throng
　We at His feet may fall!
　We'll join the everlasting song,
　And crown Him Lord of all.

No. 204. Come to Jesus.

1 Come to Jesus, Come to Jesus,
　Come to Jesus just now,
　Just now come to Jesus
　Come to Jesus just now.

2 He will save you,

3 Oh, believe Him

4 He is able,

5 He is willing,

6 He'll receive you,

7 Call upon Him,

8 He will hear you,

9 Look unto Him,

10 He'll forgive you,

11 Flee to Jesus,

12 Only trust Him,

13 Jesus loves you,

14 Don't reject Him

15 I believe Him.

16 Hallelujah. Amen.

No. 205. Come, Every Soul.

1 Come, every soul by sin oppressed,
　There's mercy with the Lord,
　And He will surely give you rest,
　By trusting in His word.

Cho.—Only trust Him, only trust Him,
　Only trust Him now;
　He will save you, He will save you,
　He will save you now.

2 For Jesus shed His precious blood
　Rich blessings to bestow;
　Plunge now into the crimson tide
　That washes white as snow.

Cho.—Come to Jesus, come to Jesus,
　Come to Jesus now;
　He will save you, He will save you,
　He will save you now.

3 Yes, Jesus is the Truth, the Way,
　That leads you into rest;
　Believe in Him without delay,
　And you are fully blest.

Cho.—Don't reject Him, don't reject Him,
　Don't reject Him now;
　He will save you, He will save you,
　He will save you now

4 O Jesus, blessed Jesus, dear,
　I'm coming now to Thee,
　Since Thou hast made the way so clear,
　And full salvation free.

Cho.—I will trust Him, I will trust Him,
　I will trust Him now;
　He will save me, He will save me,
　He will save me now.

5 Come, then, and join this holy band,
　And on to glory go;
　To dwell in that celestial land,
　Where joys immortal flow

No. 206. I Have a Savior.

1 I have a Savior, He's pleading in glory.
　A dear, loving Savior, tho' earth friends be few;
　And now He is watching in tenderness o'er me,
　And, oh! that my Savior were your Savior too!

Cho.—For you I am praying,
　For you I am praying,
　For you I am praying,
　I'm praying for you.

2 I have a Father; to me He has given
　A hope for eternity, blessed and true;
　And soon will He call me to meet Him in heaven,
　But, oh! that He'd let me bring you with me too!

3 I have a peace; It is calm as a river—
　A peace that the friends of the world never know,
　My Savior alone is its Author and Giver,
　And, oh! could I know it was given to you!

4 When Jesus has found you, tell others the story,
　That my loving Savior is your Savior too;
　Then pray that your Savior may bring them to glory,
　And prayer will be answered—'twas answered for you!

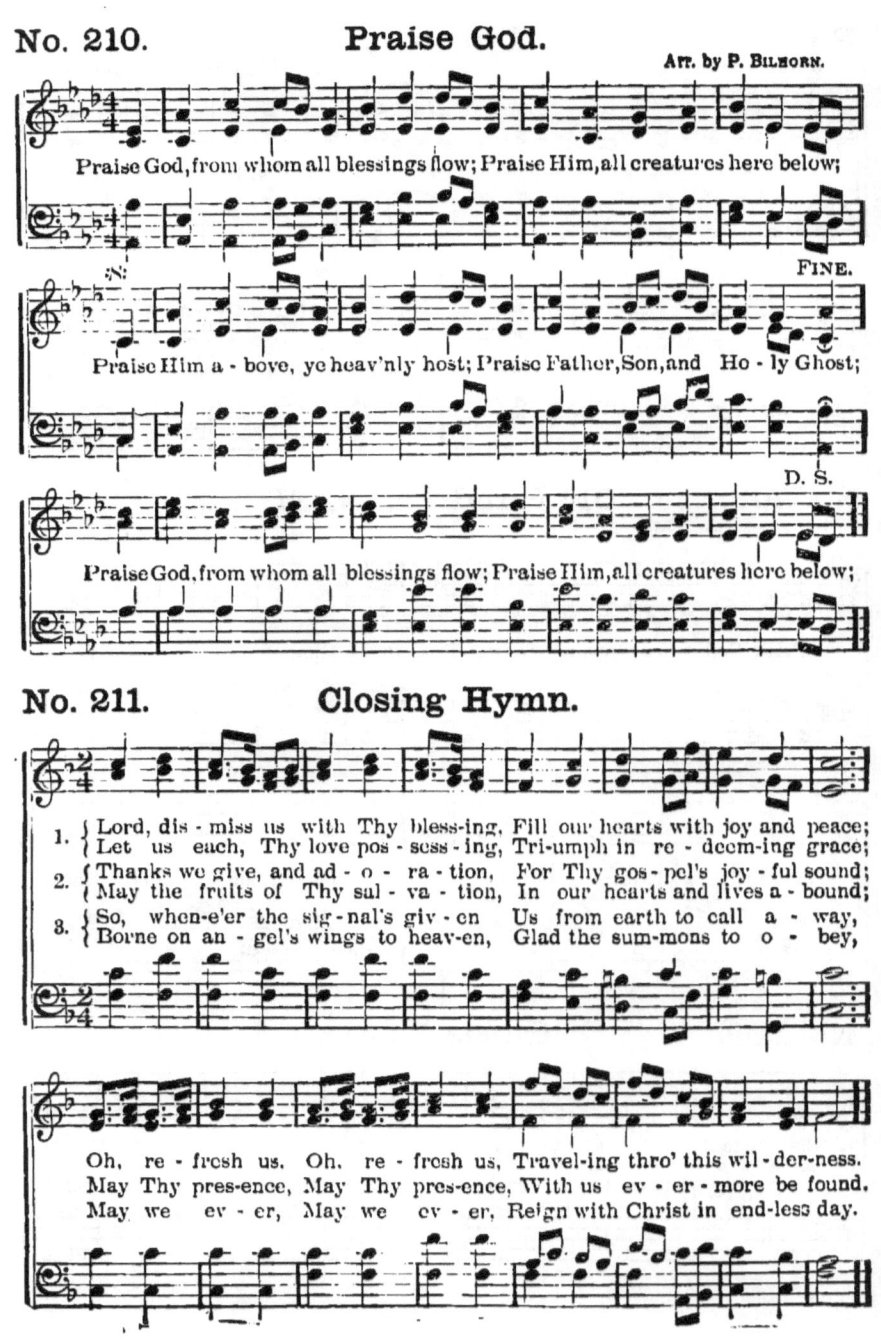

INDEX.

(NAMES OF TITLES ONLY.)

Able to Save and Keep	43
Abiding in Him	172
All Hail the Power of Jesus' Name	203
All Taken Away	114
Am I a Soldier?	197
Antioch	80
Anywhere with Jesus	44
Are You Enrolled?	157
Are You Ready?	115
Are You Washed in the.	4
Arise, My Soul, Arise	135
Art Thou Weary?	103
Art Thou Drifting?	21
A Sinner like Me	65
A Story Sweet and True	88

B

Beautiful Robes	32
Behold! a Stranger	61
Bid Him Come In	20
Blest be the Tie	190
Blessed Assurance	67
Blessed be the Name	30
Blessed Jesus, Keep Me White	50
Blessed is He that Endureth	122
Believe and be Saved	29
Bringing In the Sheaves	39
Bring Them In	62

C

Calvary	160
Cast All Your Care upon Him	170
Christ is All	99
Christ hath Redeemed Us	81
Closer, Lord, to Thee	87
Closing Hymn	211
Conquer through His Word	37
Coming To-day	136
Come, Thou Fount	191
Come to Jesus	204
Come, Every Soul	205
Come, ye Sinners	180
Cross and Crown	194

D

Depth of Mercy, Can there be	129
Do not Pass Me By	57
Doxology. (Sessions)	207
Drifting Away from God	59

E

Evening Prayer	187

F

Farewell	166
Fill Me Now	7
"For the Lord God will Help Me."	84

G

Give Me Jesus	147
Glad tidings of Joy	83

Glorious Fountain	40
Glory to Jesus, He Saves	2
Glory to His Name	38
Gloria Patri	209
God be With You	41
God be Merciful to Me. (Ps.)	90
Go Forth, Go Forth!	3

H

Hamburg. (Jesus, and Shall It.)	183
Having Done All, to Stand	132
Heaven is not Far Away	127
He Calleth for Thee	36
He is Just the Same To-day	64
His Yoke is Easy	120
Holy, Holy, Holy!	149
Holy Spirit, Guide, Revealer	72
Holy Spirit, Come In	5
Holy Spirit, Faithful Guide	119
How Can I but Love Him?	123
How Firm a Foundation	35

I

I Could Not do without Thee	173
I have a Savior	206
I hear the Savior Say	201
I Hear Thy Welcome Voice	202
I'm Bound to Enter Heaven	19
In the Morning	134
In the Hour of Trial	78
In Perfect Peace	179
In Sight of the Crystal Sea	86
Is It There, Written There?	178
Is it Well with your Soul	150
Is My Name Written There?	52
Is there One Prepared for Me?	182
It May be the Last Time	110
I will Follow Thee, my Savior	142
I Will, I Will	11
I will Sing the Wondrous Story	22

J

Jesus is Waiting	28
Jesus, Lover of my Soul	195
Jesus, have Mercy on Me	156
Jesus Saves	15
Jesus Saves Me To-day	126
Jesus Redeems Me	139
Jesus Shepherd, Lead Me	181
Jesus Tells Me	58
Just as I Am	196
Jesus, Thou my Only Refuge	104

K

Keep Us Revived	101

L

Lead Me, Savior	100
Leaning on Jesus	176
Leaning on the Everlasting Arms	66
Let the Savior In	9

INDEX.

"Let Not Your Heart be Troubled".... 124
Love Divine........................ 154

M

Marching Onward 75
Master, the Tempest is.............. 188
Martyn 163
Mercy's Free....................... 167
Meet Me There..................... 117
Move Forward...................... 63
My Country, 'tis of Thee........... 48
My Name in Mother's Prayer........ 85
My Jesus, I Love Thee.............. 8
My Redeemer Lives................. 112
My Title's Clear................... 133
My Soul, be on Thy Guard.......... 175

N

Nearer the Cross................... 27
Nearer, my God, to Thee............ 198
Nobody Knows but Jesus............ 155
"Not To-night."................... 92

O

O Day of Rest and Gladness......... 159
O House of Many Mansions.......... 130
Oh, Happy Day..................... 145
Oh, Could I Speak................. 113
Oh, for a Heart................... 169
Old Hundred. L. M................. 208
Onward, Christian Soldiers......... 16
Onward and Upward................. 77
On Jordan's Stormy Banks.......... 82
On the Cross...................... 34
Over Jordan....................... 105

P

Passing Homeward.................. 164
Pleyel's Hymn. (Hasten, Sinner.).... 76
Praise God........................ 210
Prepare Ye the Way................ 93

R

Ready and Willing to Save.......... 158
Redeemed.......................... 56
Redemption........................ 6
Revive Us Again................... 1
Rock of Ages...................... 193
Room in Heaven for Thee........... 31

S

Saved to the Uttermost............. 151
Savior, Pilot Me.................. 23
Seeking Me........................ 128
Seeking the Lost.................. 168
Shall I be Saved To-night?......... 107
Showers Refreshing................ 14
Softly and Tenderly............... 98
Soldiers in the Army.............. 47
Some Mother's Boy................. 146
Stand Up for Jesus................ 25
Standing on the Promises.......... 45
Standing, Knocking, Pleading...... 111
Steadily Marching On.............. 102
Step In........................... 73
Step out on the Promise........... 185

Sunshine in my Soul................ 12
Sweet Peace....................... 24

T

Take Me as I Am................... 161
Take my Life and Let It Be........ 141
Tell It to Jesus.................. 116
Tell It Out....................... 69
The Bird with a Broken Wing....... 89
The Best Friend is Jesus.......... 60
The Full Reward................... 96
The Great Physician............... 53
The Good Shepherd................. 125
The Haven of Rest................. 106
The Half has Never been Told...... 49
The Lord's our Rock............... 10
The Master is Come................ 95
The Man of Galilee................ 54
The Prodigal Child................ 17
The Palace of the King. (Ps.)..... 144
The Penitent's Plea............... 174
The Savior is my All in All....... 18
The Triune God.................... 33
The Voice of the Holy Spirit...... 68
There is a Fountain............... 200
There's a Wideness in............. 109
They Sing a New Song.............. 140
Throw Out the Life-Line........... 13
Trusting in Jesus Alone........... 94
To the Battle..................... 186

V

Victory through Grace............. 184

W

Waiting for the Savior............ 153
Waiting and Watching for Jesus.... 91
Walking with God.................. 74
We'll Never Say Good-by........... 46
We'll Work till Jesus Comes....... 71
We shall See Him.................. 148
We shall Know as We............... 152
We Walk by Faith.................. 55
We would See Jesus................ 138
What a Savior..................... 118
What a Friend..................... 192
What a Gathering.................. 51
What will You Do with the King?... 108
What will You Do?................. 121
What will Your Harvest Be?........ 79
When the King Comes in............ 143
When my Savior I shall See........ 26
Wherewithal....................... 177
Where will You Spend Eternity?.... 165
While Shepherds Watched........... 70
While Jesus Whispers.............. 42
Which Life shall It Be?........... 171
Who will Go?...................... 189
Why not Receive Him?.............. 137
Why Longer Wait?.................. 97
Wilt Thou be Made Whole?.......... 162
Wonderful Story of Love........... 131
Work for the night is coming...... 199

www.ingramcontent.com/pod-product-compliance
Lightning Source LLC
Chambersburg PA
CBHW020902230426
43666CB00008B/1283